God
and History
in Early
Christian
Thought

A Study of Themes from Justin Martyr to
Gregory the Great

L. G. PATTERSON

God
and History
in Early
Christian
Thought

THE SEABURY PRESS ✠ NEW YORK

ACKNOWLEDGMENTS

Grateful acknowledgment is made to the following publishers for permission to use copyrighted material from the titles listed:

Fathers of the Church, Inc.—"The Fathers of the Church" series,
    Volumes XXII and LII.
The Newman Press—"Ancient Christian Writers" series, Volume XXV.

TO MY FATHER AND MOTHER

Preface

THIS BOOK is designed as a companion to that of R. A. Norris, Jr., *God and World in Early Christian Theology* and as such forms part of a series devoted to examining the views of Patristic writers on themes of modern theological interest. Like the earlier volume, it does not claim to say anything new but seeks rather to review much recent work from one particular perspective. Its ultimate purpose is to draw attention to another of the ways in which Patristic thought reveals itself to be the watershed between the world of classical ideas and the culture of our own time.

One particular difference between this volume and its predecessor deserves special notice. It is our contention that the interests of Christianity and classical *historia* became enmeshed chiefly in the writings of Latin Christians of the period following the recognition of the Church by Emperor Constantine. The scope of our study is thus far broader than that required for the investigation of the issues raised for Christianity by the cosmological speculations of later Greek Platonism. In consequence a certain lack of symmetry is to be noted between the two works, and in the present instance a far larger body of Patristic writings needs to be taken into account than was the case in the other. As a result, it seemed proper to supplement the general bibliography with brief bibliographical notes to the various chapters. Even so, neither the purpose of the work nor the limitations of space allow scope for the kind of discussion of critical opinion which might otherwise be useful.

Drafts of the several chapters were prepared as the basis for six lectures on "Gospel and History in Early Christian Theology" delivered at the Conference in Theology for College and University Faculty, held at Trinity College, Hartford, in June, 1966. I am indebted to the leaders of the Conference for providing the incentive for the work.

I must also express my special indebtedness for much that is sound in this book to my colleague, the Rev. Dr. Harvey H. Guthrie, Jr., with whom I have regularly conducted a seminar in which many of the views offered here have been developed and revised; and to my friend, the Rev. Dr. R. A. Norris, Jr., whose extensive knowledge and exacting criticism have been available in such widely separated places as New York and Oxford, as well as on Cape Cod.

L. G. PATTERSON

Barnstable, Massachusetts
Feast of the Apostle James, 1966

Contents

*God
and History
in Early
Christian
Thought*

1

The Primitive Gospel and Classical Historia

It is a commonplace of much modern biblical study and popular Christian apologetics that history was the place where Israel believed God's purposes to have been revealed and where the Gospel announced their manifestation in the coming of the Messiah in "the last days." History, we are repeatedly told, occupied a unique place in biblical thought, whereas it was consistently undervalued or disregarded in the classical world to which the Gospel was carried in the early Christian centuries. Moreover, runs the argument, the classical influence on early Christian writers is seen in their failure to stress the radically historical character of the Gospel in their attempts to interpret Christianity to their contemporaries.

There is unquestionably a good deal of truth behind this view. Christians regarded the present course of events, part of what we should now call "history," as giving evidence that God was beginning to fulfill his promises to Israel and that the completion of his purposes was at hand. On the other hand, many of their pagan contemporaries found it difficult to invest this or any other course of events with such significance as they did. The clash of cultures in the early Christian centuries is in no small part revealed by the different views held by Christians and pagans with regard to the extent to which any specific human happenings shed light on the ultimate issue of human destiny.

The difficulty with this view, of course, stems from the fact that its use of the word "history" as referring to the totality of human happenings is peculiar to our own time. After all, *historia* is a Greek word which generally signified any "inquiry," but which had long before the advent of Christianity come to refer in particular to that effort to record human happenings which was an important department of classical intellectual endeavor. For example, it may be noted that none of the writers whose works are incorporated in our New Testament invest the word with any special significance in the course of their efforts to develop the implications of the events to which they were witnesses. And it is notorious that with the sole exception of the author of Luke-Acts they show scarcely any acquaintance with the classical discipline of *historia* as such. While it is not to be expected that the representatives of any culture will be consistent in employing even its most significant words—quite the contrary is, indeed, often the case—the fact is that the use of "history" to refer to happenings as such was as uncommon in the classical world into which Christianity was born as it is common in our own time.*

Much more is at stake here than the use of a word. To speak of biblical thought as locating God's action in "history" is to obscure the nature both of the clash of cultures in the early Christian era and of its aftermath in our own time. The question which must occur to anyone familiar with the Christian literature of the cen-

---

* English is not, of course, the only language of modern theology. The German distinction between *historie* and *geschichte,* both of which words must be rendered "history" in English, contains problems of its own. In current theological usage, it is fair to say that the former generally refers to an exact recounting of events, the latter to what is at once a truer and an intellectually revised version of those events. The distinction shows the influence of the post-Kantian philosophical situation, which is everywhere apparent in German theology. But if the German problems are more complicated than ours, they are the same as ours on the single point of their tendency to obscure the normal Greco-Latin usage. The French *histoire* and the Italian *storia* have more of the connotations of the classical *historia.* But the theological discussion which has produced the modern interest in the relation of Christianity and "history" is fundamentally Anglo-German in origin.

turies following that from which most of the New Testament writings emanate, aware as he must be of both the biblical and the classical sources of its ideas, is not that of whether this literature takes the "historical character" of the Gospel seriously. Rather, it is that of why Christians were led, in the course of their efforts to interpret their faith to their pagan contemporaries, to invade the preserve of the practitioners of classical *historia*. The answer to this question is by no means as obvious as it appears at first sight, and care in using the word "history" is necessary if its character is to be grasped. While Christians possessed a faith grounded in what was in principle subject matter for the discipline of *historia,* their evaluation of a certain course of events as manifesting the divine purpose sprang from a view of the world very different from that which had given rise to the discussion of "historical" methods applicable to the study of any and all human happenings. Indeed, we shall see that current definitions of *historia* were such as to obscure the relationship between its subject matter and that of the Gospel.

But if current references to biblical thought as locating God's action in "history" tend to obscure the relation of the Gospel and *historia* in the early Christian centuries, they also obscure its aftermath in the issues now confronting us in the relation of the Gospel to modern historiography. We are members of a culture which is at once fascinated with the realization that human life is lived within the context of the course of events which we now call "history" and uncertain as to the conclusions to be drawn from that realization. We are also faced with a historical enterprise in the stricter sense which is more aware of its origins in a revival of classical *historia* in opposition to Christian theological interpretations of the course of events than it is aware of the profound debt which it owes to the belief in God's providential action which gave rise to those interpretations. In these circumstances, frequent reference to the preoccupation of biblical thought with "history" may do something to suggest the contemporaneity of the Gospel. But it is of little help either in the task of making the claims of the Gospel clear in our time or in honest discussion with representatives of a historiography which is in such a peculiar way the stepchild of the same Christianity of which we are heirs today.

The purpose of the present work is to study the steps by which early Christian writers were led to the point where their investment in the subject matter of classical *historia* became such that they were forced to speak on issues which were "historical" in the sense that they understood the word. Its modern importance lies in the fact that the efforts of these writers form the background—if you will, the "prehistory"—of the situation in which we have now to interpret the Gospel to ourselves and others, in an age in which both the correspondence and the divergence between the Christian proclamation of God's action in the course of events still unfolding before us, and our own awareness of the eventful character of human life, are far more clearly perceived than was the case in the early Christian centuries. If we take our point of departure from what is perhaps a caricature of much modern Christian talk about "history," it is simply because such a study as we intend is in principle impossible on the view that these centuries were marked by nothing but a progressive departure from Christian concern with "history." We shall attempt to show that such a study is not only possible but that it holds the clue to the nature of the present circumstances in which the claim that Christianity is concerned with "history" seems a means of recommending the faith to modern men.

THE PRIMITIVE GOSPEL

We begin our study with some broad and perhaps inevitably arbitrary remarks on the two subjects which form its background, the emergence of the "eschatological" motif in the primitive Gospel and the development of the classical intellectual discipline of *historia*.

The Gospel which the early Christian writers inherited first appeared as the claim that certain present events marked the beginning of a final intervention in human affairs by the God who had acted in Israel's past. It called on its hearers to recognize that they were living at the end of the present age and to conduct themselves as befitted those who knew that God's kingdom or reign over his creation was already making its influence felt.

It is perhaps unfortunate that the term "eschatological" is so commonly used to describe this central motif of the Gospel. While the term is ultimately derived from early references to "the final events" (*ta eschata*) now beginning to occur, it is not easily divested of its later significance as a description of the department of scholastic and reformed theology devoted to the study of the purely future state which would follow on the end of the present state of human existence. In fact, the Gospel linked past and future in a fashion analogous to that in which the modern political analyst seeks to discern the future implications of present policies and actions. It purported to see the ultimate purposes of God already at work in the present course of events. It thus regarded these events themselves as having "eschatological" significance.

Recent light on this "eschatological" motif of the Gospel has largely come from Old Testament studies, particularly those associated with the name of Professor G. von Rad, which are concerned with the crisis that confronted Israel's faith in the aftermath of its loss of political power to the rising Neo-Babylonian empire. Israel's faith had initially taken form as a response to the events which had seen an ancient tribal amphictyony give place to a modest Near Eastern empire under David and his immediate successors. These events were regarded not merely as manifesting the purposes of Israel's God, but as virtually corresponding to his achievement of power over the divine powers of the ancient Near Eastern pantheon. The writings which form the basis of the Pentateuch and the Former Prophets (Genesis-Kings) were composed in an effort to explain these events in this sense. The collapse of the Davidic heritage under new political pressures from without, and in particular the fall of Jerusalem in 587 B.C., thus destroyed the matrix in which Israel's understanding of its relation to its God had taken shape.

It is in the light of this crisis that the Prophetic writings have to be viewed. The collapse of political power is here seen not as proving the impotence of God, but as the result of his judgment against his people. Moreover, that collapse is seen as proof of God's power over the nations who are now incorporating the Davidic heritage in a new political context; and at least in Second Isaiah the view is propounded that the sufferings of Israel serve as a witness to those nations of the issues which will confront them when God finally moves to establish direct rule over human life.

Although the influence of the Prophetic movement is discernible in the Deuteronomic editing of the earlier religious writings, done in an effort to document God's judgments in Israel's past, the movement did not provide an answer to the insistent question of the means by which God now guided the destinies of his people. One such answer was that of the Priestly writers, who undertook another revision and expansion of the earlier writings in an attempt to show that the Jerusalemite *cultus*, restored as the center of a purely religious sovereignty by the Persian inheritors of the Neo-Babylonian empire, had been designed from the beginning to be the meeting place of Israel and its God. With the Deuteronomic editors, they gave the Pentateuch and Former Prophets their classic shape.

But other answers were forthcoming. The Wisdom literature sprang from an attempt to develop the ancient notion of the inspiration of wise men into a theory of the means by which God continued to make himself accessible. Indeed, such writings as Ecclesiasticus and the Wisdom of Solomon went so far as to undertake an independent reinterpretation of the events recorded in the earlier religious writings in an effort to show that this wisdom had all along been the source of Israel's life. Nor can notice be omitted of the Apocalyptic writings, which employed a view of revelation not unlike that of the Wisdom literature in developing forecasts of the future fulfillment of God's plan to redeem Israel and to bring the nations under his rule. It was an important contribution of these writings that they succeeded, in large part with the help of imagery drawn from Persian religious descriptions of a cosmic war between good and evil powers, in articulating the element of finality in earlier Prophetic pronouncements regarding the eventual renewal of God's activity in human affairs.

In contrast to the Pentateuchal and Prophetic writings, Wisdom and Apocalyptic works had only a tenuous claim to status among Jewish Scriptures. They were finally only sparsely represented even in the compendious collections which Hellenistic Christians inherited from the synagogues of the Greek-speaking Jewish Diaspora, and which were finally incorporated in the Septuagint Old Testament. It has long been clear, however, that through these works we are introduced most directly to the forms of Jewish belief which the earliest converts to Christianity brought with them to their new faith.

Among instances in which Apocalyptic figures appear in the Lord's own teaching, we need only notice the forecasts of the issuance of the present course of events in the appearance of the heavenly Son of Man of Apocalyptic expectation (Mk. 15:62; Mt. 26:64; cf. Mt. 16:28; Lk. 22:69), and the function to be exercised by the angelic powers at the final judgment (Mk. 8:38; Mt. 16:27; Lk. 9:26). And a far larger complement of such figures is found in the elaborated pictures of the future given by the Gospel writers and other primitive Christian authors. At the same time, the pervasive influence of Wisdom ideas is evident both in the didactic character of the Lord's teaching and in the forms in which it was preserved before its inclusion in the Gospels. Indeed, such evidence as we possess of the so-called "Q" document employed by the synoptic Gospels suggests that it was virtually a collection of the sayings of a "wise man."

But our evidence of the influence of Apocalyptic and Wisdom themes on the Judaism from which the earliest converts to Christianity came ultimately serves to throw the radical novelty of their new faith into bold relief. That faith did not rest on a vision of the future or on the truth of divinely inspired teachings. It rested on certain present events which were regarded as marking the actual beginning of the final intervention of God in human affairs. The impact of that faith can be traced in the restraint with which the earliest Christians drew on contemporary Apocalyptic in the elaboration of what they took to be the future implications of present events, as well as in the extent to which their teaching was preoccupied with the concrete demand that those events placed upon men. And it may be somewhat more than merely rhetorical to note in this connection that "Q" is known to us only from the use of its material by Gospel writers concerned primarily with the meaning of those events.

The point is that the convictions of the earliest Christians regarding the renewal of God's activity in human affairs involved the abandonment in principle of the search for access to God which had given rise to the principal forms of contemporary Jewish thought. In fact their convictions harked back to an earlier stage of Israel's development, and did so not in the sense that they returned to an earlier notion concerning God's activity in general but precisely in the sense that they discerned that activity itself in the events of the present. As Professor Harvey H. Guthrie has said, the primitive Christians stand with the earliest Pentateuchal strata and with the Prophetic writers in their claim to see Israel's God at work in the events of which they were witnesses.

It is to be hoped that the reader is as aware as the writer of the limitations which necessitate leaving these observations on the background of the Gospel almost wholly undocumented. The reason for making these observations is simply that they are the easiest way of introducing a fundamental and crucial consideration regarding the Christian writings now incorporated in our New Testament. What gives these writings their coherence is not an agreement with regard to any set of abstract teachings but a commitment to the events before them as the place where God's final intervention in human affairs was beginning to take place. In fact, the study of these writings is the study of the earliest stages of a process of elaboration and revision of Christian expectations in the light of new considerations arising out of the unfolding course of events itself.

What is being offered here is an explanation of the much debated relationship between the original proclamation of Jesus reflected in the probably dominical pronouncements buried in the Gospels and the somewhat later proclamation about Jesus represented in the views of the authors of the Gospels and the other literature of roughly the latter half of the first century—what has sometimes been called the relationship of the Gospel of Jesus and the Gospel about Jesus.

It need scarcely be argued that such a classic description of the first preaching as "the time is fulfilled, the kingdom of God is at hand; repent and believe the Gospel" (Mk. 1:15; Mt. 4:17) arises from a powerful apprehension, attributable to no one but Jesus himself, of the immediate manifestation of divine power in the happenings of the present. This apprehension underlies the interpretation of the healings as proof of the limitation of the powers of the demons (Mk. 3:22-27; Mt. 12:22-29; Lk. 11:14-23). It is inherent in the appeal made to Isaiah 29:18 ff. in support of taking not only the healings but the preaching of the Gospel to the poor as proof that the "coming one," the agency in the establishment of the kingdom, is even now present to perform his redemptive functions (Mt. 11:4-6; Lk. 4:18-19). It is strikingly embodied in the predictions that many now living will witness the fullness of the divine power (Mk. 9:1; Mt. 16:28; Lk. 9:27). Such was the significance later attached to the Lord's death by the Gospel writers that it is probably now impossible to uncover Jesus' own view of the opposition which his preaching aroused in the religious leadership and its consequences for himself. But recurrent references to Israel's rejection of the prophets (Mt. 23:37-39; Lk. 13:34-35; cf. Mk. 12:10-11), employing as they do a motif of the "coming one" as Prophet unused in later interpretations of the Lord's person, suggest that he saw in them another confirmation of the truth of the Gospel. In any case, there is no evidence of any lessening of the conviction that the future kingdom of God now loomed directly over the present. The prediction that the High Priest himself would see the Son of Man come in power (Mk. 14:62; Mt. 26:64; cf. Lk. 22:69), as well as the prediction that the disciples would soon join their Lord in drinking the new wine of the kingdom (Mk. 14:25; Mt. 26:29; Lk. 13:29), assumes a future virtually continuous with the present. Much effort has been expended on the problem of the time expected to elapse before the final manifestation of the kingdom, but the resolution of this difficult point is less important than the recognition that no essential discontinuity is anticipated between the final fulfillment and the present foreshadowing of divine power. It would have been truly surprising had any been anticipated by one schooled in contemporary Jewish expectation.

It is precisely on the point of the relation of the future fulfillment and the present foreshadowing of divine power that we may turn from the preaching of the Lord buried in the Gospels to that of the Gospel writers and their contemporaries. In this connection, it must first of all be insisted that each had that future fulfillment constantly in view in all his considerations. On no other assumption do any of their assertions make sense within the world of ideas from which they came. But once this is recognized, it may be said that the preaching of the Lord's followers differs from his on the crucial point that his resurrection from death, his vindication by God after his rejection by men, had inevitably become for them the central witness to the truth of his message. It was seen as the decisive turning point in the accomplishment of God's purposes at the very same time that it gave assurance of their final achievement. Its effect was thus to introduce precisely the sort of discontinuity between the future fulfillment and the present foreshadowing of divine power which had been lacking in the original message. This discontinuity was reflected in the way in which references were now made to an eventual "unveiling" (*apokalypsis,* I Pet. 1:7) or "manifestation" (*epiphaneia:* I Tim. 6:14; II Tim. 1:10) of the Lord as the completion of a work already in principle accomplished. And the same idea is now found in references to the "emerging presence" (*parousia,* I Thess. 2:19; II Thess. 2:1; James 5:7; I John 2:28) not merely of the kingdom but of the Lord himself in his future glory. The synoptic Gospels offer fascinating examples of the imposition of this meaning of the term on sayings which originally had in view the eventual unveiling of the Lord's present authority (Mk. 13:6-27; cf. Mt. 24:3-44; Lk. 21:8-33). Indeed, while the resurrection may in some instances have been at first regarded merely as deferring his future recognition as the "coming one" (Acts 4:20-21), it soon came generally to be seen as marking his immediate achievement of that role (Acts 3:36). He was no longer simply the Christ who was to come, but the Christ who had already assumed his power.

The main point about the transition from the preaching of the Lord to that of his followers—from the Gospel of Jesus to the Gospel about Jesus—is that it is the result of a revision of the understanding of the relation of present and future forced upon his followers by the unfolding course of events which they took to be the place where the final dealings of God with his people were beginning to occur. Such was their commitment to the contemporary world of ideas that much of their time was expended in attempting to show that this course of events was precisely that which had been forecast in the Scriptures, which were now quite uniformly considered to be the repository of Israel's knowledge of the purposes of God. It was in this connection that they sought "testimonies" from the Scriptures to show that the death and resurrection of the Lord had been anticipated no less than his final manifestation in glory (Mk. 8:31; 9:12; cf. Mt. 16:21; 17:12; Lk. 9:22; 17:25; 24:26, 46; Acts 3:18; 26:23), throughout applying to him the title and style of Messiah or Christ, which he had himself found it expedient to avoid (Mk. 12:35-37; cf. Mt. 22:41-46; Lk. 20:41-44). At the same time, their confrontation with contemporary Apocalyptic speculations understandably led them to sound out the bearing of the same course of events on such speculations (Mk. 13:6-27 and parallels above, cf. I Thess. 4:13-18; II Thess. 2:1-12; Rom. 15:12-28; I Pet. 4:7-19), and even eventually to construct a Christian Apocalypse, despite the disinclination of the Lord to indulge in such forecasts (Mk. 13:32; Acts 1:7). But these developments must not be allowed to obscure the fact that it was an effort to come to terms with the implications of the unfolding course of events itself which governed their often problematical isolation of "testimonies" and their imperious acceptance and rejection of contemporary expectations of the future.

It is in this connection that attention must be drawn to the work of Paul, not only as the most influential single attempt to enunciate the implications of the Gospel in its many aspects, but as that in which new and unprecedented events continued to force their attention on the earliest Christians. Thus it was in connection with the interest of uncircumcised Gentiles in the Gospel that it fell to Paul to seek an answer to the question of the purpose of the period of time extending between the resurrection of Christ and the now certain manifestation of divine power at the end of the present age. The obvious answer to this question was, of course, that time was being given for the churches or "assemblies" (*ekklesiae*) of the elect to be formed in response to the preaching of the Gospel. For Paul, however, the lesson which the events of the present seemed to teach was that the elect were not coextensive with Judaism. The argument which he developed in defense of his own practice of admitting Gentiles to the churches without circumcision is a classic instance of the earliest Christian use of "testimonies." The "offspring" promised Abraham in reward for his faith before the establishment of the covenant of circumcision (Gen. 15:3-6; cf. Gen. 12:7; 22:17-18) is an eschatological Israel based on faith in God's promise rather than on obedience to Torah, and it is this Israel which is now being formed from Gentiles as well as Jews (Rom. 3:21-4:25; Gal. 3:1-19). In connection with this argument, Paul advanced his celebrated interpretation of Torah as having all along had the purpose merely of calling men to recognize their need of the salvation which can only come through faith in God's promise (Gal. 3:19-29; cf. Rom. 2:1-3:20). Unable to stop at this point, however, he further suggested that what was indeed already beginning to happen in fulfillment of the prophecies relating to the calling of the Gentiles and the apostasy of Israel was the calling of the elect Gentiles before the conversion of Judaism on the eve of the final manifestation of divine power (Rom. 9:1-11:36).

It was perhaps inevitable that Patristic interpreters of Paul, such as Origen and Augustine, schooled in classical reflections on human nature, would devote their attention to the psychological implications of his interpretation of Torah and so pave the way for the "Paulinism" of medieval and modern Christianity. But if we are to understand Paul himself, we must see that it was as an interpretation of present events taken to manifest the purposes of God that his views took shape. His work was another major step in the efforts of the earliest Christians to come to terms with the unfolding course of events to which their faith was so intimately bound, in contrast to that of their Jewish contemporaries.

We may bring our discussion to a close by observing that while Paul's work had much to do with determining the views of his successors regarding the place of the Church in the purposes of God, the unfolding course of events itself soon served to contradict his view of the immediate future. The abortive Jewish revolt against Rome and the subsequent withdrawal of the Jewish community within itself served to foreclose the possibility of the kind of free relations with Judaism which Paul's generation knew. Paul's prognostications regarding the calling of the Gentiles now seemed to have heralded the virtually total reconstitution of the Church beyond Judaism as the immediate goal of God's action (Mk. 13:10; cf. Mt. 28:18-20; Lk. 24:46). And the growing concern of the Roman authorities with popular unrest aroused by Christianity soon gave rise to preoccupation with the great *imperium* as the final manifestation of the powers of the present age arrayed against God but doomed to inevitable defeat (Rev. 17:1-18:24). But putting these further adjustments to one side, it is with Paul that we reach a point from which the logic of primitive Christian thought can be seen in full-blown form. It was a logic which left the way open to further revisions in the Christian understanding of the purposes of God manifest in the unfolding course of events. It was a logic which at once harked back to the roots of Israel's faith and would continue to operate in the thought of those who were to inherit the Gospel in the centuries to come.

CLASSICAL HISTORIA

The life of the age which Christians believed had entered upon its last days was dominated by the classical or Greco-Roman civilization, the product of vast and revolutionary events which had witnessed the incorporation of the ancient Near Eastern world of Israel's past in the now maritime-commercial society of the eastern Mediterranean in the wake of the conquests of Alexander the Great and the further subjugation of his successors to the rising power of Rome. If we leave momentarily on one side the Roman or Latin cultural developments of the time, we may characterize the culture of this later Greek or Hellenistic world as the product of the study of the remains of early Greek literature, science, and philosophy in the circumstances in which they had now become the intellectual meeting-ground of the many cultures which jostled one another in the strange new setting in which they found themselves. The principal intellectual phenomenon of the period was the rediscovery of the works of Plato as the most useful means of correlating the views of all past philosophical schools and of explaining the places to be assigned to all future forms of intellectual endeavor. The now vaunted revival of Platonism in the Hellenistic world was thus at once less and more than the creation of a philosophical system. While it arbitrarily imposed certain assumptions on its followers, such as the primacy of intellection over perception, the superiority of rational-spiritual over emotional-physical experience, and the identification of the former with the divine and the latter with the debased aspects of the cosmos, it established no more in principle than a series of problems for discussion by the inheritors of the Greek intellectual quest. At the same time, it not only provided the professional academicians of the time with justification for their endeavors to trace the elements of permanence observable in life but also provided the increasing number of amateur intellectuals for whom Greek culture was the clue to social and economic advancement with hope that some divine quality of human nature would survive the apparently meaningless round of daily existence. It thus came to operate as the world-view of the Hellenistic society, the explanation of its continuing rational endeavor and the substitute for its religious inheritance.

Although we shall shortly see that the circumstances of life in the Hellenistic world had an important influence on both Greek and Latin historical writing, it is not hard to see why the impact of the Platonic revival tended to divert attention from the effort to describe events which was the principal concern of *historia*. One does not need to know of Plato's strictures against those who merely catalogued human events (*Meno* 97AB), or Aristotle's association of historians with artists and poets rather than with those engaged in rational study (*Poetics* 1451B), to perceive the adverse effect which identification of true knowledge with a grasp of the permanence behind the changing cosmos would have had on the study of human happenings. In our view at least, not enough attention has been paid to the fact that the life of Greek polis itself, diverse in its development and too long preoccupied with internal class struggles for its own good, had not confronted its observers with the kind of unitive course of events which might have produced an early Greek rational equivalent to the religious interpretation of Israel's somewhat abortive rise to power among the ancient Near Eastern empires. But even so, the early Greek intellectual quest, which had its origin in efforts to find rational alternatives to religious explanations of the mingled order and disorder of existence, had from the first found little significance in the seemingly arbitrary elements in human no less than physical life. The revival of interest in that body of philosophical writings which more than any other identified reality with the order rather than the disorder in the cosmos thus proved a barrier to the prosecution of historical study in the Hellenistic world.

Despite the devaluation of historical study at the hands of later Platonism, however, the fact is that *historia* was a product of the same intellectual awakening which gave rise to philosophy itself. This is easily seen in Herodotus, whose account of the Persian War provided the impetus for all later historical work. Much time has rightly been spent on such matters as Herodotus' limitation of his method to the canvassing of living witnesses of events, or his willingness to include divine intervention as a factor in human happenings. But it should not be overlooked that when he writes that his "inquiries" (*histories*) are designed not only to celebrate the deeds of the Greeks and the barbarians but also to set forth "the cause of their going to war with each other" (*History* I.*praef.*), he states his intention to supplant mere heroic narration with the same kind of concern with observable phenomena from which philosophy took its rise.

Thucydides' account of the Peloponnesian War between Athens and Sparta, the other great example of the historical work of the early Greek period, has received particular attention for what Professor C. N. Cochrane first recognized as its use of medical theories in its diagnostic approach to the war as a disease which initially broke out among the Athenians, its invention of speeches designed to convey the issues of crucial turning points in the struggle, and other features which seem to depart from the spirit of Herodotus' exact inquiry. But when Thucydides distinguishes his work from that of the mere "record-makers" (*logographoi*) (*History* I.21.1), and explains that his methods should appeal to those who seek such nonmythological accounts of events as will aid them in understanding what is about to occur (I.22.4), he is actually making explicit Herodotus' own purposes. Indeed, Thucydides' account, seen in its wider context, is simply an effort to apply such new methods as are available to him in an attempt at a rational description of the same aspect of observable phenomena which had engaged the attention of his predecessor. It thus continues to express the same interests which preoccupied the scientists no less than the philosophers of his own time.

The period embraced by the works of Herodotus and Thucydides reveals much about the classical enterprise of *historia*. Jointly responsible though they were for the notion of *historia* as a discriminating account of contemporary events, neither was capable in practice of overlooking the fact that he was dealing with a critical turning point from which some truth about the whole life of the Greek city-states could be discerned. Similarly, while each was committed in his own way to methods designed to establish the essential truth of events—a commitment long regarded as foreclosing the influence of personal factors on human happenings— neither could finally disregard the uniqueness of the events which were the subject of his "inquiry." Thus it is that the seemingly naïve flavor of Herodotus' narrative is in large part a creation of the contrast between his own "inquiry" and his subtle recognition of the grand proportions of the conflict between the Greek city-states and the Persian empire. And by the same token, while far too much has been read into Thucydides' passing remark that a nonmythological account of events will appeal to those really concerned with what is about to occur (I.22.4), the fact remains that his diagnostic approach to the Peloponnesian War and in particular the extremes of subjectivity to which it led him in his invention of speeches were difficult to reconcile with his own perception of the decisive character of the struggle which we now know depleted the resources and shook the self-confidence of the Hellenes in a fashion which decisively affected the whole future course of Greek civilization. The fact to emerge from these considerations is not that human happenings were unimportant to the Greeks. On the contrary, it is that the lines along which they pursued their very real interest in these happenings were so determined by the approach to reality characteristic of all aspects of the Greek intellectual awakening as to leave the practitioners of *historia* chronically incapable of handling the novelty which we now take to be the central feature of the phenomena with which they dealt.

The emergence of the Greek intellectual enterprise from the quaint, domestic world of the Greek city-states into the cosmopolitan environment of Hellenistic society had its effect on all aspects of Greek rational endeavor. For *historia* in particular, the enmeshment of Greek fortunes first with those of the ancient Near East, and then with those of Rome made it hard to avoid the bearing of broader factors on the recording of events than had theretofore been admitted. For one thing, the fact that the present flowed out of and was partly explained by a past could not now be overlooked. It is not surprising that Hellenistic historians paid even less attention to the policy of limiting their work to "inquiry" into present happenings than had their predecessors. For another thing, the influence on events of such a personality as Alexander, to mention only one, combined with the growing tendency of philosophy to concern itself with human nature to suggest that individuals might have a greater place in the determination of events than had generally been thought earlier. And it is not surprising that Hellenistic historians tended to pay more attention to great figures than had their predecessors. Both the "universalization" and the "personalization" of *historia* characteristic of the period reflect the changed circumstances in which the Greek intellectual enterprise was now set.

The supreme—almost unique—example of the tendency to "universalization" is Polybius' *Universal History,* composed at Rome with the help of archival evidence concerning Rome's struggle with Carthage in the Punic Wars and her first involvements in the affairs of the dynasties established by the "successors" of Alexander. The effect of these events in broadening Polybius' understanding of his task is apparent when he asks:

> Can anyone be so indifferent or idle as not to care to know by what means, and under what kind of polity, almost the whole inhabited world was conquered and brought under the single domination of the Romans, and that too within a period of not quite fifty-three years? Or who again can be so completely absorbed in other subjects of contemplation or study as to think any of them superior in importance to the accurate understanding of an event for which the past offers no precedent? (*Universal History* I.1.)

The surviving five books of Polybius' enormous work contain observations on the contrast between the political life of Rome and the Greek city-states whose almost modern tone is precisely the result of this search for an explanation of the novel developments of the writer's time.

It has often been noticed that Polybius employs a notion of Fortune strongly influenced by the Stoic conception of the articulated cosmos as emerging from and returning to an original unity. Thus he writes that "there is this analogy between the plan of my *historia* and the marvelous spirit of the age. . . . Just as Fortune made almost all the affairs of the world incline in one direction, and forced them to converge upon one and the same point, so it is my task to [write] a compendious view of the ways in which Fortune accomplished its purpose" (I.4). But Polybius also shows the influence of the Stoic insistence on resignation in the face of change when he writes that *historia* is "in the truest sense an education and a training for political life; and that the most instructive, or rather the only, method of learning to bear with dignity the vicissitudes of Fortune is to recall the catastrophes of others" (I.1). Thus at the same time that his philosophical commitments supply him with a certain freedom to explore the novelty of the course of events, they also lead him to devalue the significance of the course of events for human destiny—a tendency which the Platonic revival was subsequently to encourage.

Polybius remained confident that political—that is, constitutional—factors held the clue to events; however, the chief example of the tendency to "personalization" characteristic of Hellenistic *historia* is the *Lives* of the amateur historian and philosopher Plutarch, in which the virtues of representative Greeks and Romans are compared, to the advantage of the former rather than of the latter. But the reason Plutarch's work is the last great product of the development of classical Greek *historia* is obvious from his scattered remarks on the nature and value of the study. In the "Life of Timoleon," for example, he observes that his interest is "to habituate my memory to receive and retain images of the best and worthiest characters," adding that "I am thus able to free myself from any ignoble, base, or vicious impressions contracted from the contagion of ill company . . . by the remedy of turning my thoughts in a happy and calm temper to view these noble examples" (I.1-2). That is, his ventures in *historia* are useful as a dimension of his personal struggle to conquer vice and develop virtue, to which he was directed by the particular combination of Stoic ethics and Platonic metaphysics—with its stress on the desirability of moderating the passions in the interests of the release of the soul —to which his fascination with the revival of Platonism in his time had led him. In effect we can say that the very interests which give Plutarch's sketches their lively personal character are those which were afterward to divert attention from what he himself still valued in *historia*. After him, the triumph of philosophy for the Hellenistic intelligentsia was virtually complete.

That triumph was not complete, however, among the Romans who inherited the historical enterprise in its Hellenistic form at almost the very moment that it had seemed to have lost its appeal among the Greeks. Indeed, it is probable that the very existence of the Roman archival material used by Polybius already reveals a Roman concern with events which encouraged the renewal of interest in *historia* on Roman soil; this we must now consider. For the fact is that this renewal was not the result of a mere perpetuation of a Hellenistic intellectual interest, but an example of a more general adaptation of Greek forms of expression by a people who were seeking to articulate a quite different understanding of reality from that which was just then coming to maturity in the Hellenistic world.

The question of the sources of Roman or Latin ideas, whether in Etruscan or other paleo-Latin cultural developments, or in response to the growth and consolidation of Roman power over Italy and Punic Africa, is an issue of too great importance to admit of summary treatment here. Various factors combined to arouse in the Latins a sense of their being a unique people upon whom events were thrusting a special destiny. In striking contrast to the early rise of religious skepticism among the Greeks was the transformation of the gods of the classical pantheon at Latin hands into powers on whose good will the success of Rome in her struggles with her enemies had depended in the past and would depend in the future. In equally striking contrast with the lack of unity among the Greek city-states and their seeming inability to avoid the dangers of class warfare was the perpetuation among Latins of a notion of the welfare of Rome as a cause in whose service each member of the society must seek his highest calling. The people who increasingly involved themselves in the affairs of the East after the Punic Wars and who finally succeeded to the heritage of Alexander the Great faced the world with a quite different set of questions about the nature of things from that which impelled the revival of Platonism among the Hellenistic intelligentsia.

And it is precisely in the shape of a series of *questions* that we encounter the Latin spirit as it was initially given expression by the Latin intelligentsia who now fell under the spell of the later Greek culture with which they were in direct contact. The fact is that the growth of Roman power had created a serious religious and political crisis. Philosophical skepticism with regard to religious polytheism made its impact on the Latins at the very time that disastrous civil wars began to make clear that the Roman government, constituted to handle the affairs of the *respublica,* was incapable of shouldering the enormous problems of ruling what Polybius called "almost the whole inhabited world." Thus the very people on whom the future of Rome depended had every reason to question whether there was a providence at work in Roman life and every reason to question the validity of service in its cause. Few of the remains of the period lack some tinge of the depressionistic introspection classically expressed in the poetry of Lucretius and Catullus; and few show any tendency to accept in undiluted form the confident assurance of later Platonism that true meaning is to be found in a spiritual stability beyond physical change.

Virtually the only confident voice among the Roman "Hellenists" of the time is that of the statesman-philosopher Cicero, who remained convinced that philosophical ideas could be enlisted in defense of service to the *respublica.* In his *On the Commonwealth* (*De republica*), a dialogue modeled on Plato's work of similar title and claiming to be a discussion of the virtues of citizenship by members of the circle of Scipio Africanus the Younger, Cicero undertakes to discuss not what the ideal commonwealth might be, but how Rome had emerged out of the past as that ideal commonwealth in being, "by a route which we may call the way of nature" (II.15.29). The Roman constitution, indeed, fulfills all the "wise provisions for that association of citizens in a happy and honorable life" which is the purpose of a commonwealth (IV.2.2). Its disruption is attributable to the fact that "our desires (which) are hard masters over our thoughts . . . urge to every sort of crime those whom they have inflamed by their allurements" (VI.1.1). The implication is clear that those who have regard for the immortal nature of the soul (VI.3.3) will find defense of the commonwealth the means of thwarting the passions which seek to distort human life (cf. I.38.60).

The Latin outlook of Cicero is evident in the peculiar way in which he fuses an appeal to Rome's emergence to greatness with various elements drawn from a Platonic-Stoic philosophical anthropology which saw the conquest of the passions as the means of perfection of the soul. But it also is evident in the fact that the work is something more than an abstract argument. The "Dream of Scipio" which stands at its end (IV.10.9 ff.), in a comparable position to the "Myth of Er" in Plato's work, describes a divine revelation to Scipio of the truth of the argument that service to Rome is the means of the soul's eternal glory. Moreover, by carefully setting the dialogue on the eve of Scipio's own death in the service of the *respublica* (129 B.C.), Cicero intends to issue a compelling call to his contemporaries to accept for themselves the truth which made Scipio famous. This particular feature of the work—and it is one which we shall see repeated in both pagan and Christian Latin writings more than once—is an easily overlooked witness to the profound difference between the Latin understanding of sources of human action and that embodied in the intellectual appeal characteristically made by Greek authors.

In the event, however, it was not by a revival of faith in the meaning of the old constitution but by the instilling of hope in the possibilities of the reforms instituted by the adopted nephew of

Julius Caesar, Octavian, or Augustus, that the crisis of the time was at least temporarily resolved. And it was in the celebration of "the Augustan peace" by such poets as Horace and Vergil that the call to find fulfillment of life in service to Rome was issued on grounds which Cicero did not foresee. Vergil's epic poem *Aeneid* commands attention here as the supreme example of the work of a Roman "Hellenist" who saw in the accomplishments of Augustus the achievement of Roman destiny. As Professor Brooks Otis has shown, Vergil's revival of the epic form, long disused and regarded as unusable in Hellenistic literary circles, enabled him to identify Augustus' work as the providential outcome of a vast course of events. Roughly following the structure of the Homeric *Odyssey*, Vergil begins by locating Aeneas, the legendary founder of Rome, who had escaped from the sack of Troy at the hands of the very Greeks over whom Rome was now sovereign, at Carthage midway on his journey to Italy. By this means, he is able to introduce the theme of overarching destiny into a properly mythological epic account of the struggles through which Aeneas has arrived at the seat of Rome's traditional enemy, Punic Carthage (I-III). Against this background, Vergil now sets Aeneas' profound internal struggle between love for Dido, the Carthaginian queen, and his dim awareness of the necessity of fulfilling his destiny (IV). At last obedient to a divine command to leave Carthage (V), Aeneas experiences on the shores of Italy what the skeptical Vergil is careful to call a *dream* of the underworld, in which he not only encounters past heroes who have found or lost purpose in life by obeying or disregarding their destinies, but also envisions what can now be a more circumstantial account of the glorious future which will unfold as a result of the founding of Rome (VI). It is thus out of "the love of what would come" (VI.889) that there is born the stalwart or *pius* Aeneas of the succeeding part of the work (VII-XII), who conquers primitive Latium in a struggle described with heroic effects reminiscent of the Homeric *Iliad,* and so opens the way for the civilized era of world peace and security now forever established by Augustus.

The similarities between the Augustan Vergil and the Republican Cicero are easily recognized. Here again a Roman "Hellenist" issued a call to his contemporaries to support the destiny manifest in the growth of Roman power. And here again that call was issued through the setting forth of a person—Aeneas, but also the Augustus whom he foreshadows—in whom is seen the effect of knowledge of that destiny as the means of conquering base concerns in the interest of achieving human greatness. It was Vergil's special accomplishment to have devised a means of describing that destiny in its full dimensions without abandoning his intellectual integrity. Subsequent events were to reveal that the Augustan *imperium* was less than a perfect instrument of world peace and security. But Vergil's work stands as a unique witness to the kind of proclamation which alone could provide an answer to the questions about the nature of things which the religious and political crisis of the *respublica* raised for the Roman "Hellenists."

The renewal of interest in *historia* among the Roman intelligentsia is itself a witness to the Latin preoccupation with these questions as we have already seen it in Cicero and Vergil. But the work of the great Roman historians themselves must be judged on the basis of their own special adaptations of the Greek intellectual discipline to which they had succeeded. This is the case with Sallust, a younger contemporary of Cicero who joined him in supporting the old constitution. Sallust's fascination with the work of Thucydides is evident in the fact that, while his account of the revolt of the Punic guerrilla leader Jugurtha against Roman rule dealt with events which occurred before his own birth, both his study of the abortive *coup* of Catiline at Rome and the material treated in his lost "histories" were limited to events which he himself witnessed. In his own words, he intended to deal with the affairs (*res gestae*) of the Romans by "selecting such portions as seemed to me worthy of record" (*War with Catiline* IV.2).

The Latin outlook of Sallust is seen in the broader interest which informs the self-imposed episodic form of his work. When he speaks in philosophical terms not unlike Cicero's of the disastrous effects of passions which have been let loose from the control of reason (*War with Jugurtha* II.1-4, III.2-3; *War with Catiline* I.5-7, III.4-5), he is clearly referring to the concrete events which seem to him to have brought ruin on the *respublica* on which his hopes had been lodged. It is his generally unexpressed sense that he was witnessing a progressive corruption of Roman affairs which communicates itself in the strangely portentous character of Sallust's work, in which he searches to uncover the operation of the personal defects of the characters who he believed had such an unsettling effect on his times.

Analogous features are found in Livy, a younger contemporary of Vergil and as much the historian of the Augustan achievement as Sallust had been of the Republican tragedy. What remains of Livy's massive *From the Founding of the City* is as clearly in violation of the principle of contemporary *historia* as is Polybius' work. In Livy's case, however, this violation owes its origin to an interest in placing the present greatness of Rome in the kind of perspective which no Latin would have denied that it required. At the same time, the preface to the work makes clear that the author does not accept the providential interpretation of Roman power common in his time. "If any people ought to be allowed to consecrate their origins and refer them to a divine source," he admits, ". . . the nations of the earth may well submit to [the claims of Rome] with as good grace as they submit to Rome's domination." For himself, however, he will show how "with the gradual relaxation of discipline, morals first gave way as it were, then sank lower and lower, and finally began the downward plunge which has brought us to the present time, when we can endure neither our vices nor their cure." The value of studying these events, he concludes, is that "you may choose for yourself and your commonwealth what to imitate" among examples which he concedes include much that is honorable (*Praef.* 7-13).

Livy's remarkably contradictory statement combines the perspectives gained from the Augustan achievement with a version of the philosophical-ethical themes of Greek *historia* in a work which in its own way sees itself as issuing a call to rise to the challenge of the time not unlike that of Vergil. If it fell short of Vergil's work through its distrust of the notion of providence, it nevertheless initiated the theme of the dangers lurking in Roman greatness which was to be a rallying point in difficult times to come.

The controversial figure among the great Roman historians is Tacitus. A representative of the conservative opposition to the Augustan achievement, Tacitus' historical work is a programmatic illustration of his view, most clearly stated in his *Life of Agricola* and his *Dialogue on Oratory*, that Augustus' feigned restoration of the *respublica* actually curtailed the freedom of expression which was the source of Roman character. Tacitus' later-named *Histories* and *Annals* of Augustus' successors in the Julian dynasty have been not unfairly criticized as sensational catalogues of imperial vice and intrigue. In another sense, however, these sardonic works embody in a unique way the very concern which Tacitus shared with Sallust and Livy in the sources of Roman moral strength. Moreover, he no less than they was concerned to see his works as a call to action—though perhaps to an action which he could define less concretely than they—and in this way exemplified a characteristic which the historians shared with all other members of the Latin intelligentsia of the time. And it must be added that if his negative stance with regard to the events of his time frees him from the necessity of asking what is the meaning of the growth of Roman power, his works too are witnesses to the inbred sense of a destiny which he himself regarded as being forfeited by those whose actions he described.

The Latin phase of classical *historia* is easily summarized. The writers we have touched upon, whether historians or not, have no sense of an opposition between the attempt to describe events and the search for the meaning of existence such as had been created in the Hellenistic world. On the contrary, both the philosopher Cicero and the poet Vergil actually cast their ideas as interpretations of events which are the stuff of *historia*, while a concern similar to theirs with the events of Rome's rise to power is the obvious cause of the fascination of the Roman historians with their adopted discipline. At the same time, the Roman historians were restrained by what we have called the chronic limitations of their discipline from recognizing any historical significance in that concern as such. They were at their best when they could devote themselves to attacking religious interpretations of the Roman past or to analyzing the collapse of moral standards in the Roman present. It was when engaged in these tasks that their adaptations of Greek *historia* were of most use in the continuing Latin search for the clue to Roman greatness.

THE GOSPEL AND HISTORY

The various lines along which our investigation must now proceed are already suggested by the two subjects we have discussed. The Gospel entered the classical world as a message about the course of events which we should now call history. To proclaim that Gospel in the classical world would not necessarily or immediately involve a discussion of the subject matter of *historia* as the early Christians and their pagan contemporaries understood it. This would be true especially in the Greek world, where the chief issue would be to state the claims of any course of events to ultimate significance and where *historia* defined itself in a way that strictly precluded the providential interpretation of events. But it would be true also in the Roman world, for the simple reason that Christians regarded the events with which the Latin mind was preoccupied, and which accounted for the special interests of the great Latin historians, as belonging fundamentally to an age fast approaching its end.

But there is another side to the picture. Should the course of events to which the Gospel pointed involve Christians in new ways with the broad course of human happenings, it is not hard to see that the logic inherent in the Gospel itself would lead to further reflection on the unfolding purposes of God. Just that kind of involvement was the result of the acceptance of Christianity by the imperial government of Emperor Constantine and his successors. And it was in the aftermath of this surprising turn of events that the subject matter of *historia* became of necessity a matter of theological concern.

To consider the Christian understanding of history in the early Church is thus to study both the interpretation of the course of events on which the faith of the early Christians rested and the concern with the stuff of *historia* to which it finally led.

2

The Gospel and Later Greek Platonism: Justin to Origen

IT MAY SEEM strange to make the Greek Christian writers of the period from Justin Martyr in the middle of the second century to Origen in the middle of the third the point of departure for this study. The recurrent fascination of these writers lies chiefly in the fact that their work marks the initial confrontation of the Gospel and later Greek Platonism. As a result of their efforts to deal with the rational implications of the Christian proclamation, the cosmological and anthropological issues which underlie much of the theological reflection of the early Church began to take shape. In short, these writers are of interest precisely because of their grasp of the importance of the very intellectual concerns whose revival had taken place at the expense of the Greek historical enterprise. We shall see that their work mirrors the contemporary devaluation of *historia* rather than showing any tendency toward its renewal under Christian auspices.

It is precisely in its preoccupation with later Greek Platonism, however, that the work of these writers is of importance for us. This would be the case even on the once current view that this preoccupation was merely a regrettable departure from the norms of Christian faith, since its results color the thought of the entire era with which we are concerned. But in fact these writers had no intention of abandoning the belief that the events before them marked the final stage of God's dealings with his people. It was at their hands that there took shape the institutions—particularly the Symbol of Faith, or Creed, and the body of Christian Scriptures —in which that belief was enshrined. And it was in the interest of establishing the implications of that belief that they were led to adopt positions with regard to the philosophical speculations of their pagan contemporaries.

In tracing the persistence of this belief in these writers, therefore, we encounter the novel phenomenon of the elevation of a particular course of events to a matter of *rational* concern. It is a phenomenon without parallel in the Christian no less than in the pagan world of ideas. At the same time, we also encounter evidence of how difficult it was to reconcile the Christian evaluation of the significance of that course of events with the assumptions underlying contemporary cosmological and anthropological ideas. It is as a record of the mingled success and failure of these writers to effect such a reconciliation that their work provides the starting point for the study of early Christian reflection on the events in which God's purposes were manifested.

JUSTIN MARTYR AND HIS SUCCESSORS

The attention of the Greek Christian world of the second century was to a considerable extent centered on the Greek-speaking Christian community flourishing amid the polyglot oriental population of the imperial capital—the Roman Church. This community had become the symbolic focus of Christianity with the dispersal of the Jerusalemite Church in the course of the Jewish revolts against Rome. It possessed the apostolic tombs of Peter and Paul as witnesses to the confrontation of the Gospel and the increasingly hostile pagan empire. While it was a western outpost of what was still a fundamentally Greek religious movement, its very existence seemed to embody the issues of the time. It is not surprising that both the Christian dualist Marcion and the Christian Gnostic Valentinus sought to recommend their teachings there, or that it left its impress on the creedal, scriptural, and liturgical developments of the time.

It is important to establish the character of the second-century Roman Church, because in the middle of the century this Greek-speaking community was the setting for the beginning of the confrontation of the Gospel and later Greek philosophy in the work of Justin Martyr. This is not to say, of course, that the influence of philosophical ideas is not apparent in earlier Christian writings. The wide dissemination of such ideas in the Hellenistic world left its mark on the Judaism of which Christianity was born no less than on the other oriental cultures incorporated in the Eastern Mediterranean society. Nor can it be denied that the cosmological and anthropological assumptions of the Platonic revival are discernible in such philosophical forms of Christian Gnosticism as that of Valentinus and his disciples, both in their picture of a cosmos constituted of spiritual and physical elements, and in the use they make of the theme of self-knowledge as effecting assimilation of the human to the divine spirit. But these and other influences to one side, the fact remains that in the attempt to state the claims of accepted Christian belief in terms intelligible to the representatives of the major philosophical schools, Justin holds a special place. It is in his work that the issues which were to dominate the minds of the pioneering period of theological endeavor first begin to take shape.

It is also important to take some account of the institutional developments in which the Roman Church was implicated. While Justin shows a knowledge of at least the constitutive elements of the Symbol of Faith (*First Apology* XXII.1; XXIII.2; LXI.3) and uses the term "president" (*proestōs*) to describe for pagan readers the functions of a bishop in the Eucharist, his work antedates the elevation of Christian works to the status of "scriptures" which was already accorded the Jewish sacred writings. This does not mean that Justin is unaware of the existence of many of the writings later included in this category and still later defined as a "New" in contrast to an "Old" Testament. Indeed, his references to the Gospels as "memoirs" (*apomnēmoneumata*) of the apostles (I.66.3;

67.3) may already reflect the influence of that pagan interest in literary classics which was to be so important in both the formation and the interpretation of the Christian "canon." But the very imprecision which often makes it difficult to be certain which particular Christian writings Justin knew serves to point up the contrast between their position in his mind and that occupied by the Jewish "scriptures." In this respect, Justin—and the Roman Church of his day, supposing him to reflect it on this point—still clung to the view of the authors of the New Testament themselves that past "testimonies" had foreshadowed present events. Insofar as Justin's so-called "typological" approach to the Jewish writings, which he characteristically refers to under the general heading of "prophets" (XXIII.1; XXX.1-LV.8), departs from that of his predecessors, it is in his meticulous concern to find scriptural anticipations of present events—a concern derived from his pagan literary interests, or dictated by Marcionite and Gnostic handling of these writings.

Justin's view of the Scriptures is far more than evidence of a certain stage in the evolution of a specific Christian institution— the canon. The clue to the essential structure of Justin's theology is to be found in his assumption that Christians are witnesses to the events which mark the beginning of the fulfillment of God's promises to Israel. This is clear from his *First Apology*, which is his comprehensive statement of Christian teaching in the face at once of pagan criticism and of the imminent possibility of new legal restrictions against Christianity. In defense of the claim that Christians are not atheists, but worship the divine creator (*dēmiourgos*) through the Christ who is the manifestation of his creative Word (IX-XXIX), he argues that Christians have concrete evidence in support of their claims regarding Christ:

> We do not put our trust in mere hearsay, but are forced to believe those who prophesied [these things] before they happened, because we actually see things that have happened and are happening as was predicted (XXX.1).

And later, in elaborating the argument that the Scriptures indeed anticipated contemporary events, he comments on the text "For the

Law will go forth from Zion" (Mic. 4:2-3; Isa. 2:3-4) as referring to the spread of the Gospel which is occurring in his own time:

We can show you that this has really happened. For a band of twelve men went forth from Jerusalem, and they were common men, not trained in speaking, but by the power of God they testified to every race of mankind that they were sent by Christ to teach to all the Word of God: and now we who once killed each other not only do not make war on each other, but in order not to lie or deceive our inquisitors we gladly die for the confession of Christ (XXXIX.2-3).

And later still, in another comment on the scriptural anticipations of present happenings, he describes this age as one in which

Jesus Christ, who was crucified and died, rose again and, ascending into heaven, began to reign; and on account of what was proclaimed by the apostles in all nations as [coming] from him, there is joy for those who look forward to the incorruption which he has promised (XLII.4).

But if Justin employs the theme of the fulfillment of God's promises in defending the truth of Christianity, he also employs it in issuing his own challenge to its opponents. If things which have already happened were prophesied, he argues, then

it must similarly be believed that those things which were similarly prophesied and are yet to happen will certainly take place. . . . For the prophets foretold two comings [*parousias*] of Christ—one, which has already happened, as that of a dishonored and passible man, and the second, when as has been foretold he will come from heaven in glory with his angelic host, when he will raise the bodies of all men who have already lived, and will clothe the worthy with incorruption, but send those of the wicked, eternally conscious, into eternal fire with the evil demons (LII.2-3).

The question of the future bliss or future doom of those who oppose Christianity, he concludes, rests entirely on their own decision:

If what we say seems to you reasonable and true, treat it with respect —if it seems foolish to you then despise us as foolish creatures and do not decree the death penalty, as against enemies, for those who do no wrong. I have said before that you will not escape the future judgment of God if you continue unjust, while we will cry out, "What God desires, let that be done" (LXVIII.1).

There is doubtless a touch of bravado in the final note that Christians can accept whatever the immediate future holds as the will of the God who will finally bring them salvation, while those who seek their death are doomed even if they are carrying out God's purposes in so doing. But it is not for that reason to be discounted. It is an authentic expression of the confidence which flows from Justin's belief that God's purposes are manifest in the present course of events.

This isolation of the theme of the present and future fulfillment of God's promises will not, of course, be mistaken for an attempt to separate one aspect of Justin's thought from the rest. In the first volume of the present series, for example, Professor R. A. Norris has discussed Justin's efforts to correlate a Christian understanding of the relation of God to his creation (*genesis*) with current philosophical attempts to distinguish what is "ungenerated" (*agennētos*) in the cosmos from what is "generated" (*gennētos*). The result of these efforts, and in particular of the necessary but difficult identification of God as the "sole-ungenerated" (*Dialogue with Trypho* V.4), was, as Norris rightly sees, to initiate a discussion of the acceptability for Christians of the philosophical identification of the "generated" with what is physical and mutable and hence undesirable and even evil. But Justin's ventures onto philosophical ground also include an attempt to correlate a Christian view of the purposes of God manifest in the present course of events with the current philosophical understanding of the human problem: the view that the development of the rational and spiritual element in man's nature—that which he shares with the divine—is impeded by the passions which arise in him because of the irrational and physical element which he shares with the lower animals. It was in this area that Justin paved the way for a discussion of the acceptability to Christians of views of man which curtailed human responsibility for sin and instead emphasized the disastrous effects of embodied existence—a discussion of no less importance than that of "generated" existence. But what must not be overlooked is that this discussion had its origin in an effort to state the meaning of the concrete events which marked the final phase of God's dealings with men.

Justin's correlation of the Christian understanding of present events with a philosophical view of the human problem is already apparent in his assertion in the *First Apology* that those who oppose Christianity are in the grip of an "irrational impulse" (*alogos hormē*, I.3) and an "unreasoning passion" (*alogos pathē*, V.1). Justin attributes their condition to the work of the evil demons who seek to forestall the accomplishment of God's purposes (*First Apology* XIV.1-2), but the terms which he employs make it clear that he sees that work as involving the distortion of the rational element in man. Similarly, Justin's invitation to his readers to recognize what is "reasonable and true" (LXVIII.1) as clearly combines a call to avoid God's condemnation at the last judgment with the assertion that Christianity is the means to the perfection of that rational element. Thus philosophical ideas are fused with Christian belief in Justin's understanding of the circumstances to which he addresses himself in this work.

But the *First Apology* reveals the presence of this fusion at the very heart of Justin's thought in the place which it assigns to the emergence of Greek philosophy in its account of God's plans for the salvation of men. Justin's views arc partly a development of— and are certainly rendered more plausible by reference to—contemporary Jewish correlation of claims for the antiquity of Moses with the old tradition of Plato's visit to Egypt. This combination of ideas had already provided Philo with the notion of Plato's dependence on Moses which informs his Platonic interpretation of the Torah. But while Justin shows acquaintance with such ideas (LIX.1-6), his own views are markedly different in that they regard the work of God in Christ both as the fulfillment of the promises of God recorded in the Scriptures and as the perfection of the philosophical quest. Far from simply justifying a Platonic interpretation of the Scriptures, these ideas suggest to Justin that the philosophers have played an important subordinate role in the preparation of men for Christ.

The outline of Justin's argument is easily stated. It was, he thinks, the same divine Word, the agent of God in the creation of the cosmos (XXI.1; XXIII.2; cf. *Second Apology* VI.1-2; *Dialogue* C.4), who both foretold his appearance to the scriptural authors (*First Apology* XLVI.2-4; LXIII.1-3) and inspired Socrates and the Platonists in particular to recognize that it was through his appearance that men would be saved (*First Apology* V.3-4; *Second Apology* X.1-8). But it is not so easy to grasp precisely what his argument signifies with regard to the fashion in which the appearance of the Word in Christ fulfills the expectations of both the Scriptures and philosophy. The implication of his position is certainly that Christ is the bearer to men of the truth which the Platonists sought as the means of the soul's perfection, and some such notion is clearly in his mind when he attributes to the philosophers a certain share in the divine Word and argues that they were themselves persecuted in proportion to their grasp of the truth (*Second Apology* VII-X). At the same time, however, he is content to take the incorporation into fellowship with Christ in baptism and the Eucharist as the means of preparing believers for the incorruption to come (*First Apology* LXV.1; LXVI.1).

The fact is that neither the quality of Justin's mind nor the circumstances in which he found himself were such as to lead him to clarify this point. Thus in the famous, so-called autobiographical, statement of the path along which an educated man will be led to espouse Christianity, it is sufficient for him to argue that even the Platonists have failed to grasp that a "generated" soul is neither possessed of immortality nor capable of immediate knowledge of God in order to suggest these have now been made available through Christ (*Dialogue* II-VIII). His argument is of interest not only because it involves the revision of a number of philosophical themes in the light of the conviction that God is "sole-ungenerated" but also because it assumes that the defects of "generated" existence are somehow overcome through Christ. Precisely why this should be the case is not, however, a question which he is compelled at the moment to treat directly or at length.

It is easy for us, as we look at Justin from the perspective provided by later discussion of the philosophical view of the human problem, to see how many difficulties are inherent in his confident assertion that the defects of "generated" existence are conquered in Christ. It is perhaps less easy, just because of our interest in Justin's contributions to that later discussion, to grasp the crucial point that Justin's view depends for its cogency on his assumption that God's action in the present course of events is at once the fulfillment of his promises to Israel and the goal of the Greek philosophical quest. In fact, it was as one who reflected upon the purposes of God manifest in those events in the light of the insights of philosophy that Justin must be understood if the nature of the issues which he bequeathed to his successors is to be fully appreciated.

Even though he was himself a student of philosophy rather than of *historia*, Justin can scarcely have been ignorant of the Greek historical classics; and at one point he adorns his remarks on Christian willingness to face death with the account in Xenophon's *Memorabilia* of Hercules' rejection of the immediate pleasures of Vice in favor of the call of Virtue to a hard life with an incorruptible reward (*Second Apology* XI)—this in order to add pagan to Christian precedent for his views. But it should be clear that the issues which confront Justin in his interpretation of God's purposes manifest in the present course of events are not such as to lead him into any discussion of the theological significance of *historia*. In fact, his use of Xenophon is interesting precisely because it draws on material which has no bearing whatever on what the Greek historians regarded as the subject matter of their study.

Justin's lack of interest in *historia* is evident in the several instances in which he actually uses the verb "to inquire" (*historein*) in fashions which suggest that he is familiar with the principles of the classical discipline itself. Thus in attacking supposed parallels to the resurrection of Christ in pagan mythology which might serve to discount its uniqueness, Justin says that pagans "relate" (*historōsi*) the resurrection of Bacchus, Zeus' son (*Dialogue* LXIX.2). Again, in referring in a quite different connection to the text "Let us make man . . ." (Gen. 1:26), he speaks of the words as those which Moses "related" (*historēso*) himself (LXII.2). Vague as these references are, they show an association of the verb in question with the recording of real or alleged events in what the authors of such records intend to be an accurate fashion. It is just because he so understood the enterprise that he saw little relation between it and what he believed to be the truth about the issues of the present.

It is solely in connection with the irrelevance of *historia* to the issues which Justin's belief in the action of God in present events created for him that we must deal with Justin's immediate successors, his own disciple Tatian and the more remote figure of Theophilus of Antioch. Both are of great interest for their contributions to the discussion of the Christian approach to the human problem which Justin's work precipitated. While Tatian finally became identified with Gnosticism, his suggestion that man fell under the domination of the passions because of the loss to the soul of the truly rational element—the mind (*nous*) of contemporary Platonic anthropology—which is the source of its communion with the divine Word (*Address to the Greeks* XII.1) had an important bearing on later attempts to employ the Platonic trichotomous anthropology (body, soul, and mind), which Justin had only vaguely mentioned (*Dialogue* IV; *Second Apology* X.1), in an effort to explain the human condition in terms which require the decisive action of God for its betterment. Similarly, Theophilus not only clarified at least some of the philosophical implications of Justin's view of God as "sole-ungenerated" (*Letter to Autolycus* II.5), but also, in his explanation of man's recovery from his original disobedience as analogous to the growth of a child in wisdom (the so-called "childhood analogy"), he sought an independent way of relating Christian understanding of the action of God to the common philosophical theme of the discipline needed for the perfection of the soul (II.25-27). As in the case of Justin himself, however, Tatian and Theophilus are confronted with the philosophical rather than the historical implications of their faith.

The more frequent references of these writers to *historia* show more clearly than Justin's vague allusions the minor place which the discipline was likely to occupy in the work of the Greek Christian writers of the period. Thus Tatian is spurred largely by attacks on the inaccuracy of the Scriptures (*Address to the Greeks* XL.1) to claim that *historia* is actually among the arts which the Greeks learned from the Egyptians (I.1), that Moses was the earliest of the historians (XXXI.1), and that the chronological errors of the Homeric "histories" are owing to the inferiority of Greek efforts to employ the discipline (XXXI.4). Tatian's claim follows the same lines as the Jewish arguments for the antiquity and superiority of the sacred writings mentioned in connection with Justin's work. But while this claim looms larger in Tatian's mind than in Justin's, it does so as a counter to the charge of the intellectual poverty of Christianity rather than as a matter of theological interest.

Theophilus' even more elaborate references to *historia* occupy much the same place in his thought. In developing further his claim for the antiquity and accuracy of the Scriptures, Theophilus actually ventures to demonstrate that they are "more ancient and true than those of the Greeks and the Egyptians, or any other historians" (*Letter to Autolycus* III.26.1), by contrasting their accurate information about such events as the deluge with the vagueness of other records (III.16-19) and by establishing their chronological priority to those of pagan writers (III.20-29). Moreover, in explaining the silence of the Greeks regarding the scriptural "histories" he magnifies Tatian's charge that the Greeks are culturally inferior to the point of saying that their impiety as well as their recent acquisition of learning is responsible for their failure to recognize the actions of the true God (III.20). But while Theophilus thus proceeds even further than Tatian along the path pursued in such Jewish writings as Josephus' so-called *Treatise against Apion*, his argument is scarcely more theological in its implications.

The factors at work here become much clearer in the references made to *historia* by Athenagoras, the isolated figure who possessed the widest acquaintance with and deepest appreciation of contemporary intellectual movements among the Christians of the time. In attacking pagan polytheism, Athenagoras not only adopts arguments drawn from contemporary philosophy, but also asks, with his characteristic irony, what evidence there is in the "histories" of Kronos, Zeus, and Koré to indicate that they are gods (*Plea for the Christians* XX.3). Indeed, he later asserts, the pagan priests have conspired to hide from men the fact that these "histories" actually reveal the gods to have been mere men (XXVI.1; cf. XXVIII.3). The point is that Athenagoras abandons—if he was aware of—the common Jewish and Christian attempt to defend the antiquity of the scriptural "histories" and concentrates on exploiting the possibilities provided in the assumptions underlying the efforts of historians to arrive at an accurate account of human events. It is for this reason that *historia* is at once less important to him than to his Christian contemporaries and more useful to him than to them as a weapon in the struggle with the pagan intelligentsia.

Athenagoras' few remarks provide an essential clue to the peculiar position of *historia* in the writings of his contemporaries. It was easy enough to identify the Scriptures as "histories" and useful to defend their antiquity and accuracy against the peripheral charges of the pagan intellectuals. But in fact *historia* was fundamentally a recounting of human events which discounted efforts to explain them by reference to divine causes. Jews and Christians might glibly refer to tales of the doings of pagan gods—as well as to accounts of the work of their God—as "histories." But in fact this was loose talk. The reason why *historia* had failed to attract the attention of Hellenistic culture was that it did not concern itself with what lay behind the purely human aspects of existence, and it was for this same reason that it could finally play only an apologetic role even for those who, like Justin and his immediate successors, sought to unravel the purposes of God manifest in the course of events. This is notably the case with Justin, just because he was himself responsible for a novel interpretation of these purposes which included the development of the philosophical quest within the scope of God's purpose. But it is also the case with such Christian adaptations of Jewish apologetics as we have seen in the work of Tatian and Theophilus. Since the future discussion of the theological issues raised by these figures was to lie with Christians who were even more closely related to the world of Hellenistic culture than was Athenagoras, it is not surprising that they were to be even less concerned than he with the bearing of *historia* on the theological task as they understood it.

IRENAEUS

The work of Justin and his immediate successors did not, however, pass directly into the hands of those who were prepared to deal with the issues which it raised. It was mediated to them through the writings of another great theological figure associated with the Greek-speaking Roman Church of the second century—that of Irenaeus, bishop of the Christian community in the Gallic commercial town of Lyons in the latter part of the century. Irenaeus' monumental *Refutation of What is Falsely called "Knowledge"* (generally referred to as the treatise *Against Heresies*) is the work of a person who found himself almost literally at the western outpost of the Greek Christian world, a "resident among the Keltae and . . . accustomed for the most part to use a barbarous dialect" (*Against Heresies* I. *praef*.3). Nevertheless, this work came to embody what successive generations of Greek Christians took to be the central and distinguishing features of Christian belief. To a considerable extent, it was at Irenaeus' hands that the results of the initial efforts to establish correlations between Christian teaching and contemporary philosophical ideas became part of the common Christian heritage.

Irenaeus' place in the development of Greek Christian theology is an ambiguous one. He was not as well acquainted with the thought of the philosophical schools as his predecessors had been, and in fact he was deeply suspicious of philosophy as such. As the title of his work indicates, it was composed to attack the teachings of the Gnostic sects regarding the perverse creation of an evil physical world by beings far removed from the true spiritual God, and the redemption from it of a spiritual elite through the gift of "knowledge" (*gnōsis*) from the true spiritual God—teachings which claimed to come secretly from the apostles themselves. While the question of the origins of Gnosticism remains in dispute, the philosophical ingredients in the form of Valentinian teaching with which Irenaeus was particularly concerned were as obvious to him as they are to us (cf. II.14). It is not surprising that Irenaeus' work is pervaded by an antiphilosophical spirit. Indeed, the main purpose to which Irenaeus devotes himself after an initial effort to reveal and ridicule the secret pictures of the cosmos given by various Gnostic teachers (I-II), is to establish that the apostolic writings do nothing more than to elaborate the simple Rule of Faith (or *truth*) committed by the apostles themselves to the bishops of the communities which they established (III.1-4). The implication is clear that further speculation is both unnecessary and dangerous.

Ironically, however, Irenaeus himself had much to do with paving the way for the resumption of the discussion between Christianity and philosophy on a broader scale than before. His very effort to dispute Gnostic views of the contents of the apostolic writings, which his generation now regarded as "scriptures" on a plane with the Jewish sacred writings, had the effect of making those contents the subject of academic discussion rather than of curtailing such discussion. Moreover, Irenaeus' own interpretations of the apostolic writings led him to impose upon them certain results of the work of predecessors. For one thing, he not only accepts the now common view of God as "sole-ungenerated" but, in a startling combination of Platonic metaphysical and Aristotelian epistemological themes, proceeds to attack Gnostic speculations about the spiritual realm behind the physical cosmos by insisting that the "ungenerated" is a spiritual unity impenetrable to the human reason, which is limited to the study of physical diversity

(II.3.1-2, 7.1-9.2, 15.3). It is certainly in part for this reason that he finds it difficult to discuss the "generated" Word and invokes in his behalf Isaiah 53:8: "Who can declare his generation?" But the subject could not be so easily dismissed by his successors.

Equally important, however, is Irenaeus' use both of Theophilus' "childhood analogy" between the development of man and the growth of an infant to maturity (IV.38-39), and of Tatian's speculations regarding the loss of "mind" through Adam's disobedience (V.6-9). Both of these notions function at various stages of his elaboration of his view of Christ as "recapitulating" or "heading-up again" (Eph. 1:10) a human race at once capable of obeying God as Adam was not and possessed of the "image and likeness" to God which Adam had lost (I.10.1; cf. III.21.10; IV.38-39; V.6-9). This "recapitulation theory" served Irenaeus as a means of countering Gnostic efforts to distinguish man's physical formation from his final spiritual perfection. But it had the effect of leaving his successors with an interpretation of the Scriptures which embodied at least some features of earlier efforts to correlate Christian belief in the action of God in the course of events and a philosophical understanding of the human problem. In this area no less than the other he virtually ensured the resumption of the very speculations which he himself regarded with distaste.

Irenaeus' lack of interest in *historia* is doubtless due largely to his position on the edge of the world of Hellenistic intellectual ideas in general. But more than this is to be discerned in his silence. Unwitting though it may have been on his part, he was involved in preparing the way for a renewal of the debate with contemporary philosophy in which accounts of human happenings as such were not likely to play any significant part. By the very fact of his reading into his scriptural interpretations certain of the cosmological and anthropological views of his predecessors, he made inevitable what proved in the event a far more radical attempt to establish the relationship between God's purposes manifest in the course of events and philosophical ideas of the world and man within it than had yet been forthcoming. It was to be an attempt in which the effort to discern God's unfolding purposes, which was still evident in Justin's treatment of the rise of Greek philosophy, was increasingly to give way to more characteristically philosophical preoccupations.

CLEMENT OF ALEXANDRIA AND ORIGEN

To anyone familiar with the developments of Hellenistic culture, there is a certain inevitability in the fact that the great intellectual center of Alexandria forms the background for the renewal of the concerns of Justin and his successors in the first half of the third century. During the brief appearance of Clement as catechist of the Alexandrian Church and the longer tenure of the office by Origen during the early phase of his spectacular theological career, this Christian community witnessed a dialogue between Christian and pagan intellectuals which was never thereafter to be matched for its freedom and originality. It is common to speak of Clement and Origen as together forming an "Alexandrian School." In fact they were very different both in their temperament and in their actual teachings. What united them was a common set of issues—the issues which such truly sophisticated students of philosophical ideas as they themselves were would be bound to raise regarding the adequacy of the efforts of their predecessors to define the relation of Christianity to the philosophical enterprise.

Clement has relatively little to say about the cosmological problem created for Christians by the connotations of materiality and mutability attaching to the notion of "generated" existence—a problem exacerbated, as we have already seen, by the fact that Christian insistence on God as "sole-ungenerated" necessitated ascribing "generated" existence to the Word. While Clement occasionally refers to the Word as "generated," he tends to avoid the subject altogether and even to avoid the title "Word" itself in favor of such alternatives as Wisdom and Son (cf. *Exhortation to the Heathen* I; *Instructor* I.2; *Miscellanies* V.3; VII.2-3). Indeed, his efforts to link the Word with the divine "Mind" (*nous*) are pointed enough to suggest to some that he sets two divine beings, Mind and Word, between God and his creation (cf. his reference to the Word as "Son of Mind" in *Exhortation* X). But whatever is to be concluded on this score, the central point that Clement is not easily reconciled to the idea of a "generated" Word as the best way to describe the point of contact between God and the rational structure of the cosmos (*Miscellanies* II.11, 19). Incidental as his remarks on this subject are, they serve to reveal the new awareness of the implications of philosophical ideas already embedded in Christian teaching—in this case of the necessity of taking account of the distinction of the spiritual and rational from the physical and perceptible elements within the "generated" cosmos, which is the Alexandrian "touch."

It is the question of salvation which is, however, Clement's absorbing interest and the source of his most drastic revisions of earlier Christian teaching. Clement's point of departure is already seen in the use of the Platonic theme of the perfection of the soul through knowledge evident in the very scheme of his principal writings. In his *Exhortation to the Heathen* (*Protrepticus*) he first seeks to confront pagans with the possibility of finding access for the soul to its divine source through Christ. In his *Instructor* (*Paedagogus*) he then sets forth the discipline through which Christ allows the soul to curtail the passions which restrain its growth to perfection. Finally, in his *Miscellanies* (*Stromateis*, perhaps best rendered "Gatherings") he seeks to convey an impression of the "true knowledge" (*alēthēs gnōsis*) which belongs to the soul which has begun to achieve perfection through Christ. In practice Clement seems to have made little effort to develop his views in accordance with this plan, but the scheme itself serves to indicate the source and character of his revisions—or "clarifications," as he doubtless thought them—of earlier Christian teaching. For him, the coming of Christ has opened the way for the spiritual and rational assimilation of the soul to the divine ground of spiritual and rational life as the Platonic revival conceived it.

Clement's thought is presented so allusively and unsystematically that it defies simple description. However, some of its tendencies appear in the revision which certain of Irenaeus' ideas in particular undergo at his hands. Thus he follows Irenaeus in seeing man as originally imperfect and only truly formed in God's "image and likeness" (Gen. 1:26) through Christ (*Against Heresies* IV. 38.1); but he insists that "some" are in error in thinking that this formation takes place with reference to the corporeal structure (*Miscellanies* II.22; cf. VI.12-16). On the contrary, he asserts, it is the soul which is originally formed in the "image" of the Word and subsequently achieves "likeness" through the exercise of its rational faculty. Again, when he alludes to the famous Irenaean *dictum* usually rendered "God became man that man might become divine" (cf. *Against Heresies* III.10.2, 19.1; IV.33.4, 11) as "The Word of God became man so that you may learn from man how man may become divine" (*Exhortation to the Heathen* I), the very alterations which he makes show that he has in mind not the gift of incorruption which Irenaeus had in view but the achievement of rationality through the curtailment of the passions which is enshrined in the very scheme of his writings. At these and other points where Clement alludes to the work of his predecessors he assumes that they were speaking of that actualization of the goal of the philosophical quest which he believed was being made possible through Christ.

The great hidden problem raised by Clement's renewal of the effort to establish the relation between Christianity and the philosophical tradition was that the tendency of current philosophical reflection on the human problem was to locate the source of the passions that restrained the perfection of the soul in its possession of the body, which tied it to the physical and mutable cosmos. Clement was kept from facing this problem directly by his adoption of the Stoic theme of the passions as a sickness within the soul. But in passage after passage of his work, as in his likening of the work of Christ to that of a physician who cures "those who are diseased in body" and who himself "regulated the soul by wisdom and temperance, and tempered the body with beauty and proportion"

(*Instructor* I.1-2), it is apparent that it is to the circumstances of embodied life that he naturally tends to attribute the confusion of the soul. His virtual omission of reference to the resurrection of the body stands as mute witness to the fact that the restoration of embodied life was at once unnecessary to his view of salvation and difficult for him to accommodate to it.

This last consideration is especially important for us because it is in the course of his efforts to explain the dangerous characteristics of embodied life that Clement is led to make such observations as he thought necessary regarding the course of events which had issued in the establishment of the Christian life. Thus, in a major departure from the work of his predecessors, he abandons the "childhood analogy" of Theophilus and Irenacus and speaks of man in his original state as a young animal bereft of reason and dominated by the passions (*Instructor* I.5, 13; III.12). In a sense this departure is simply occasioned by Clement's preference for the Pauline description of Christians as regenerate children of Christ: "Being baptized," he observes, "we are illuminated, we become sons," and later he adds that "since knowledge springs up with illumination, shedding its beams around the mind, the moment we hear we who were untaught become disciples" (*Instructor* I.5-6). It takes only a little reflection, however, to see that the notion that true humanity is achieved by freeing the soul from the passions which are occasioned by man's similarity to the animals governs Clement's selection or rejection of these inherited themes.

But it is in connection with his defense of marriage against the excessive asceticism of certain Gnostics that Clement develops his understanding of God's purposes at greatest length. The divine command to "be fruitful and multiply" (Gen. 1:28) was given as the means by which man should cooperate with God in the formation of the plenitude of human beings, and it is not to be abrogated until that plenitude is achieved (*Instructor* II.10, 23; cf. *Miscellanies* III; VII *passim*). Hence, even though God has restricted the gratification of the sexual appetites through the Torah (*Instructor* II.10; *Miscellanies* III.12), the admittedly disturbing practice of marriage cannot be abandoned even by the Christian seeking the perfection open to him (*Miscellanies* VII.12). The theme of the achievement of the human plenitude had already been introduced by Irenaeus (*Against Heresies* II.3.3, 5; cf. 8.1). But its isolation and development by Clement are plainly dictated by his concern to explain why it is necessary for man to involve himself with the most dangerous of the pursuits in which one seeking to avoid the passions could possibly engage. In effect, while Clement is alert to the denial of the goodness of the physical creation inherent in Gnostic practices, he is forced to concede that it is in the circumstances of embodied life that the source of the passions is to be located.

Speculative though Clement's treatment of marriage may seem to us, we should be able to recognize that it is an attempt—and finally an unsatisfactory attempt—to deal with a fundamental problem which was bound to face anyone seriously concerned with the relation of Christianity and contemporary philosophy. That is, while Clement may have scored a victory in his specific dispute with his Gnostic opponents, he actually laid bare the more difficult question of why the soul needs to be a participant in embodied life at all. We shall see that this was a question which did not escape the attention of Origen, who granted it the fully radical treatment which it deserved.

But we cannot fail to recognize that in his treatment of marriage Clement also offers—at least by implication—his general view of the issues underlying the inauguration of the Christian life. The conclusion to be drawn from his remarks is that, while he is entirely preoccupied with explaining that event, the very terms in which he seeks to explain it are such that he is unable to give more than an abstract meaning to the concrete happenings to which his predecessors had ascribed unique significance. It seems almost extraneous to note that Clement accepted without reservation the notion that much of Plato's thought was derived from Moses (*Miscellanies* I.14-15; V.14), or that he sought to establish the greater antiquity of Moses' work by a comparative study of Greek and Hebraic chronology (I.21). The fact is that a really serious grasp of the contemporary philosophical understanding of the human problem would appear, on the basis of Clement's evidence, to involve crossing over into a world of ideas in which it was difficult to invest any specific course of events with unique significance. With Clement at last the tension between Christian belief in God's action and the assumptions underlying the philosophical tradition emerges in its true proportions.

The precise relationship between Clement and Origen remains obscure. Origen's notorious failure to mention the man whose student and successor he was is perhaps due to his disapproval of Clement's flight from Alexandria in the Severan persecution. But it is unlikely that Origen—more theologian than intellectual, more rationalist than *littérateur*—was ever a disciple of Clement in the strict sense. Their fundamental relationship lies simply in the fact that Origen addressed himself with unique lucidity and candor to the issues which Clement had only dimly discerned in his efforts to meet the challenge of philosophical ideas.

Origen's treatment of the Scriptures is not only central to any study of his work but of particular importance for us. With him for the first time the whole body of Christian and Jewish writings was conceived to be a single collection of inspired writings containing in a New and an Old Testament the unique revelation of God to man (*On First Principles* I.*praef.*; IV.1; cf. *Commentary on Matthew* II in *Philocalia* VI). But this decisive development in the formation of the scriptural canon is indistinguishable from Origen's acceptance of allegorical methods, already used by Philo and traceable to Hellenistic attempts to find philosophical meanings in classical Greek literature, for uncovering the true spiritual meaning behind the obscurities and inconsistencies of the literal sense (*Principles* IV.2.1-3.5; cf. *Homilies on Jeremiah* XXXIX in *Philocalia* X). Indeed, Origen regards the study of the Scriptures as itself the divinely appointed means of salvation. Progress in uncovering the spiritual meaning of the text is a mark of the growth of the soul in the knowledge which is its perfection (*Principles* I.*praef.*; IV.2.6-7). The astounding subtlety which characterizes all of Origen's work is seen in the manner in which he thus manages to enlarge on Clement's Platonic notion of salvation as the growth of the soul to perfection in the same breath that he makes the most exalted claims for the uniqueness of the Christian revelation. But the point should not be missed that, while Origen here opens the way to a broad consideration of the scriptural record of God's actions, he has irretrievably committed himself to the view that those actions consist in the provision of knowledge for the soul. With him, the link which continued to tie Justin and his immediate successors to the original notion of those actions as significant in themselves is strained even further than it is in Clement's unconscious disregard of the circumstances leading to the inauguration of the Christian life.

The fashion in which Origen employs his principles in practice is evident in his handling of the prickly subject of the "generated" nature of the Word, which had been bequeathed him by his predecessors—notably by Irenaeus and Clement. In developing his so-called "eternal-generation" doctrine he accepts the necessity of dealing with scriptural texts (esp. Prov. 8:22; Wisdom 7:26; John 1:1-2; I Cor. 1:15) which could not be understood in any other way than as teaching the "generation" of the Word. But while he thus sets himself a purely exegetical task, he seeks to resolve the difficulties which such texts had created for his predecessors by the subtle philosophical expedient of isolating the notion of the "generated" as the dependent from the connotations of physicality and mutability which were commonly attached to it. Thus it is conceivable to him that the divine Word is a spiritual being "always being generated" (*aei gennētos*) by God and thus free from the limitations of "generated" existence as it was generally understood (*Principles* I.2.2; IV.4.2; *On Jeremiah* IX.4; *On John* I.16-22). Despite its exegetical character, then, Origen's solution to the problem of the "generated" Word involves a peculiar revision within what is the essentially Platonic scheme of perennial relationships between cosmological principles.

Origen's views in this crucial area already begin to illustrate his peculiar function in the development of Greek Christian theology—which is that he had more to do with drawing attention to the problems which he so clearly perceived than with winning support for his highly sophisticated solutions to those problems. In the particular instance in question, attention immediately centered on the typically candid speculations in which Origen extended his view of the perpetually "generated" Word to comprehend the possibility of a perpetually "generated" cosmos (*Principles* I.4.5; cf. e.g. Methodius, *On Created Things*). Only later, in the course of the vast and complicated Trinitarian controversy, was it focused on the implications of his view of the Word itself. The much discussed question of the extent and character of these speculations cannot obscure the function of the *aei gennētos* as such in determining the place of the man who was not only at once "first of the biblicists *and* greatest of the Platonists" but also "first of the orthodox *and* greatest of the heretics."

This instance of Origen's implementation of his principles—and their effect—is chiefly of interest to us as it sheds light on the fashion in which he seeks to resolve the question of the purpose of the embodied life of the soul—the question that had led Clement to make his passing remarks on the subject of the course of events which had issued in the establishment of the Christian life. Origen's answer, cast in the form of his so-called "double creation" doctrine, is entirely scriptural in the same sense as is his solution to the problem of the "generated" Word. The answer involves him in interpreting the scriptural account of God's purposes in his dealings with men along lines similar to those found in the tractate "Poimandres" in the *Hermetic Writings*. Thus he argues that the true account of those purposes discernible behind the literal text of the Scriptures teaches that God originally created a perfect number of minds or rational natures (*logikoi*), that these for some reason turned from God and were tainted with varying degrees of evil, and that the order and diversity of the physical cosmos are explained as the result of God's efforts to provide these souls, now existing as angels, heavenly bodies, or men, with bodies commensurate with the various degrees to which they have departed from him. Through the strengthening provided by the temptations of embodiment, however, these souls will ultimately be restored to their original unity and purity, and it is as stages along the way to their restoration that God has revealed the Torah to Israel and then opened the way through Christ to an anticipation of the life which will be finally realized at the "fulfillment of all things" (*apokatastasis tōn pantōn*). Enunciated in what was perhaps a premature fashion in the early treatise *On First Principles* (i.e., on the "basic" teachings behind the Scriptures), this general scheme constitutes the thread which ties together the vast collection of Origen's commentaries and homilies on the scriptural texts themselves (*Principles* I.5-8; II.1-2, 8-9; III.5-6; IV.3.11-12; cf. esp. *Homilies on Genesis, Exodus, Numbers, Song of Songs* etc.).

Origen's answer to the question of the purpose of embodied life is, of course, no more naïvely scriptural than his solution to the problem of the "generated" Word. Indeed, with the simplicity characteristic of his most subtle efforts to deal with great issues, Origen contrives to maintain *both* the Christian insistence on the goodness of the physical cosmos *and* the philosophical view of its inappropriateness for the soul by making it a regrettable expedient arising out of God's loving concern for his creatures and a means of their restoration to their lost perfection.

The destiny of this aspect of Origen's work was much like the other. It is hard to read his work now without recognizing that he himself saw the serious problems inherent in his views, both regarding the actual cause of the defection of the disembodied rational natures (*Principles* II.9.1-2), and regarding the place to be assigned to the resurrection of the body in his scheme (*Selections on the Psalms* in Methodius, *On the Resurrection, Against Celsus* V.14-23). But in fact not even his more intelligent critics grasped the rationale behind his views. He was in general understood to have taught that an evil body was responsible for the corruption of the soul—the very position which he himself had striven so hard to avoid—and pilloried for having sought to restore Gnosticism to favor. Once again it was Origen's function to alert people to the questions with which he wrestled rather than to win a hearing for the highly sophisticated solutions he proposed to them.

For our purposes, it is important to note that, whatever else is to be said about it, Origen's "double creation" doctrine does not abandon the theme of God's purposes manifest in the course of events, even though it might at first sight seem to do so. On the contrary, his solution to the problem of embodied life is one which sets the very formation of the physical cosmos itself within the context of a peculiarly vital account of the true course of God's providential work—the work which is now going on through the illumination of souls by the Scriptures and will culminate at the final *apokatastasis.* The tension which we have seen in Clement between this central theme of Christian belief and the claims of philosophy is not expressed here in the rejection of that belief for some other. It is, rather, felt in the fact that the true picture of God's activity, as Origen believed he could discern it by allegorical study of the Scriptures, differs drastically from the literal account through which he had to pierce to discover it. Origen did not deny the truth of the literal account. But the real issues to which he believed God was addressing himself were very different from those which governed the visible affairs of men.

Origen's references to *historia* are instructive in this connection. While he several times speaks of an allegorical *historia* pointed to in the Scriptures (*On John* II.1; cf. *On Jeremiah* V.15), he more commonly follows Justin and his successors in counting the Jewish and particularly the Mosaic writings as *historia* (*Principles* IV.2.6, 8, 9; IV.3.4) where it is the literal account which he has in view (*On John*, frag. 20; *On Jeremiah* XIX.14). Set in the context of his own thought, the mere continuation of this tendency has the effect of widening even further the gulf separating the methods and matter of *historia* from the study of the true actions of God in behalf of his creatures.

We cannot leave Origen without mentioning the famous passage in which he agrees with the pagan Celsus that if all Romans worshiped the true God they would "subdue many more pursuing

enemies than those that were destroyed by the prayer of Moses"
(*Against Celsus* VIII.69). The passage is important as reflecting
the assumption regarding the earthly benefits of true worship held
in common throughout the ancient world. But it must not be overlooked that it is Celsus' own attack on Christians for neglect of the
state deities which calls forth Origen's reply, or that Origen later
states cryptically that it is really the "men of God" who are responsible for the permanence of earthly things (VIII.70). Origen may or
may not be referring here to his own view of the origin of the physical cosmos. In either case, his notion of the ultimate destiny of the
"men of God" and the means adopted by God for achieving it is not
such as to invest earthly happenings with supreme importance.

With Origen we reach the end of the pioneering phase of
Greek Christian theology. His work and that of Clement paved the
way for the theological harvest of the fourth and succeeding centuries: the mature cosmological reflections which flowed from the
Trinitarian controversy and the elaboration of the nature of the
Christian life in the light of the growing monastic institution of
that later time. But it was in the light of new responsibilities created by the formation of the Christian empire and with a sobriety
and caution painfully learned from the experience of the Alexandrians that the harvest was gathered in.

GOSPEL AND PHILOSOPHY

The Greek Christian writers from Justin to Origen
cannot be understood or judged by reference to some norm of scriptural teaching supposed to have been available to them, or on the
view that the cosmological and anthropological problems they faced
were unreal or imaginary. Theirs was the task of explaining the
Christian proclamation of the near end of the present age in the
midst of a world of ideas which would have had every right to be
heard even if it had not already left its mark on the minds of those
for whom that proclamation was designed. Their views are con-

tributions to a developing theological enterprise which is inexplicable except as an effort to show how God's action in the course of events provides answers to the problems debated in the philosophical schools regarding the world and man within it.

Once this is said, however, it must also be observed that the direction which the thought of these writers took is a witness to the increasing difficulty of that enterprise as it drew closer to the sources of contemporary philosophical ideas and began to encounter their full significance. The fact is that the cosmological and anthropological discussions of later Greek Platonism took place in the light of assumptions about the world and man very different from those which underlay the Christian proclamation of the unique significance of the events in which Christians discerned the final phase of God's dealings with his creatures. In consequence, these writers were led progressively away—not from belief in the concrete action of God as such but from that effort to discern his true purposes from the unfolding course of events which had engaged their first-century predecessors. Indeed, Justin stands alone as attempting to continue that effort in the light of his understanding of the importance of the rise of the Greek philosophical quest.

The incidental attention paid by these writers to *historia* is in its own way positive evidence of the circumstances in which they found themselves, since their progressive recognition of the depth of the cosmological and anthropological issues which they faced was part of a deepening understanding of a world of ideas in which the mere account of human happenings seemed to have little to do with the issues of human nature and destiny. This was not the case, however, among those who inherited the work of these writers within the Latin society of the western Mediterranean—and who had to confront, not the claims of philosophy but the views of the past and the expectations of the future which had been bred out of Rome's rise to world domination.

3

The Gospel and Roman Eschatology: Tertullian and Cyprian

IT IS NOT the least importance of our study of the difficulties encountered by Greek Christian writers from Justin to Origen in their efforts to expound the purposes of God to the world of philosophical ideas that they throw into sharp relief the ease with which their Latin Christian contemporaries became involved in a conflict between their own belief in those purposes and the providential view of Rome's rise to world domination current in Latin paganism. It is to this conflict—a conflict, if you will, between Christian and Roman "eschatology"—that we must now turn our attention.

The initial penetration of Christianity into the Latin society is a nice commentary on the isolation which a sense of Roman greatness and a distaste for anything conceived to be Greek or "oriental" had combined to create. From its probable beginning from Greek Christian communities in and around the metropolis of Carthage, Latin Christianity appears to have spread along the inner lines of communication linking Africa ("Africa" in the contemporary sense of the heavily Latinized provinces of the western Mediterranean littoral) with Spain and Gaul. It is not until the third century that we have more than isolated instances of the association of Latins with the Greek Christian center at Rome, and the terms "Latin" and "Roman" have separate meanings in Christian circles even into the following century.

It must not be supposed, however, that Latin Christians ever thought of themselves as belonging to a separate—Latin—Christianity. It was an equally important aspect of their pagan Latin inheritance that they understood their commitment to Christ as placing them within a new course of events flowing from his work and radically different from that in which they had stood as citizens of Rome. Nor were they fundamentally different from pagan Latins in accepting the intellectual formulations of their Greek contemporaries. Indeed, as in the case of the Roman Hellenists of an earlier time, the novel features of their thought are to be discerned in the adaptations which they were led to make in the ideas that they inherited.

Two Latin writers of the period of persecution inevitably command attention before all others. The first is Tertullian, lawyer-presbyter of the Carthaginian Church at the turn of the third century, whose singular distinction it is that his influence survived to form the mind of Catholic Latin Christianity in the period despite his own acceptance of the claims of the Montanist sect to possess a special "eschatological" gift of the Spirit. The second is Cyprian, martyr-bishop of Carthage at the middle of the century, who is no less notable for having applied the teachings of "the master" Tertullian to the situation in which he found himself confronted by another outbreak of sectarianism in the Novatianist movement. It is by studying the adaptations which forms of Greek Christian teaching—in particular, those of Justin and Irenaeus—underwent at the hands of Tertullian and Cyprian that the nature of the confrontation of the Gospel and Roman eschatology become clear.

TERTULLIAN AND THE SPIRIT
OF LATIN CHRISTIANITY

Among the many writings of Quintus Septimius Florens Tertullianus, the *Apology* and the treatise *On Prescriptions of Heretics* most clearly reveal the spirit of Latin Christianity in its earliest phases.

Although Tertullian wrote his *Apology* at a time when the illegality of Christianity against which Justin argued had been established for some half century, he begins his work on the same note as his predecessor. Christians are guiltless of the only substantial charge brought against them—that of atheism—since they merely repudiate gods which educated men have all along recognized as false (X-XI). Christians in fact worship "the one God, he who by his commanding Word . . . brought forth from nothing this . . . world," and to whom all men bear witness, even though otherwise led astray by "depraved customs . . . lusts and passions . . . [and] slavery to false gods," when they call out to him in sleep or sickness as a "testimony of the souls by nature Christian" (XVII). Tertullian's argument, elaborated in his *On the Testimony of the Soul,* is reminiscent of that employed by Cicero (*On the Nature of the Gods* II.2-5). In general, however, he follows Justin in the broader point of associating Christianity with philosophical skepticism regarding polytheism.

The novelty of Tertullian's work is, however, already apparent in his reformulation of Justin's theme as ground for attacking Rome's overt sinfulness. In what is virtually one long rhetorical question, he asks why Rome then allows human blood to be shed —in the very city founded by Aeneas—in the name of the false gods (IX), or persists in its beliefs even when both the Greek historians and Latins such as Severus and Cornelius Nepos have shown them to have been men (X), or prefers these deities not only to Socrates and other wise Greeks but to virtuous men like Cato, Pompey, or Scipio (XI). It is "the crowning guilt of men," he observes in bringing home the point of his argument on the testimony of the soul, "that they will not recognize one of whom they cannot possibly be ignorant" (XVII). Tertullian here combines the theme of philosophical skepticism with another of Justin's themes, that of the demonic character of polytheism. But his interest here is not in the exploration of these themes as such. It is in weaving from them a graphic picture of the guilt of Rome, which has refused to acknowledge the true God and allowed itself to be exploited by the false gods. As in the case of Cicero and Vergil, it is not so much the novelty of his ideas which distinguishes Tertullian's argument from that of his Greek contemporary as it is his effort to use those ideas in the description of the concrete circumstances in which his readers find themselves. We shall encounter more than one instance in which this effort explains the form given to inherited ideas in Latin Christian writing.

A new phase of Tertullian's work begins when he undertakes to explain that the Scriptures which Christians read are a "written revelation" which God has added to the testimony of the soul in order that man "seeking may find, and finding believe, and believing obey" (XVIII.1). It was, he is careful to point out, to righteous men "worthy to know the most high and reveal him" that God delivered the task of recording "his judgments by floods and fire, the rules appointed for securing his favor, as well as the retribution in store for . . . [those] ignoring them" (XVIII.3). He claims antiquity for these Scriptures, "since with you, too, it is a kind of religion to demand belief on this ground," though he adds that the establishment of their antiquity would require more study of "the histories of the most ancient nations" than Josephus undertook in his controversy with the Greeks (XIX). Such study is unnecessary, however, in view of the truth of the Scriptures evident in their accurate forecasting of present events—and even of the catastrophes which the pagans currently attribute to the displeasure of the pagan gods over the rise of Christianity:

> Nor need you wait long or look far to discover [that the scriptures are divine]. The things which will teach you are before your eyes: the world, the present age, the issues of events. Everything which happens was foretold; whatever we see was announced. The earth swallows up cities. . . . Civil and foreign wars convulse the earth. . . . The humble are exalted and the proud brought low. Justice grows rare; iniquity multiplies. . . . Now all this was predicted and written down before it happened. While we suffer these evils we read about them. While we examine the scriptures they are verified. . . . (And) hence we possess a firm faith in coming events as already proved for us because they were announced along with what we see day by day fulfilled (XX).

Christianity's claim to truth, Tertullian continues (XXI),

rests not on its antiquity but on the fact of its having been foretold by God. For when the Jews proved unworthy of his trust, he undertook to fulfill a purpose already announced—that of extending his work among the Gentiles through Christ. As the Jews should have recognized,

the holy oracles which predicted their destiny had always also announced that among the final phases of this age (*sub extremis curriculis saeculi*) God would select more faithful worshippers from every nation, people, and place, upon whom he would confer more abundant grace because of their capacity for more adequate discipline. Therefore one appeared among us whose coming to renovate and illuminate men had been announced by God —that is, Christ, the Son of God (XXI.6).

Thus it is that, while the Jews still refuse to recognize that a first as well as a final coming of Christ is announced in their Scriptures, the pagans have the opportunity of drawing the proper conclusion from the life and works of Christ and of abandoning their false gods and the oracles which seem to support them.

Tertullian's dependence on themes which we have already encountered in Justin's work is as clear here as it was before. The notion that the truth of Christianity can be established from the fulfillment of the prophecies found in the Scriptures is Justin's, and it is noteworthy that Tertullian retains the essential form of this argument even though he commonly follows the practice of designating Christian as well as Jewish writings as Scriptures. Moreover, the argument that the fulfillment of some prophecies guarantees the future fulfillment of others is equally Justin's, though Tertullian does not actually lay the stress which Justin does on the judgment which the future holds for the persecutors.

But the novel use to which Tertullian puts these themes is equally clear. While he certainly holds out little hope for the persecutors, the very fact that he does not pursue Justin's argument serves to reveal his preoccupation with the possibilities now actually open to men of "every nation, people, and place" through the coming of Christ. It is this preoccupation which creates the vivid sense of the present action of God and distinguishes his form of Justin's argument from its more academic original. Moreover, while Tertullian speaks of Christ's coming to "renovate and illuminate" men, the effect of his work is conceived as opening the way to obedience to God's will—that they may "believing obey"—rather than to the redemptive knowledge which the Alexandrian teachers were beginning to stress in Tertullian's own time. Tertullian's understanding of the human condition is developed in his treatise *On the Soul*, in which contemporary philosophical ideas are employed to assert that human fulfillment is to be found in the achievement of virtue through the conquest of the passions which beset the soul when contact with the divine nature is lost (cf. XI-XIII; XXXVIII-XLI). But here, in the *Apology*, the issue is more directly stated by saying that a righteousness greater than that which the Jews once possessed is now being made available to those who accept the "more abundant grace" given through Christ. Indeed, Tertullian's views are once again reminiscent of those of Cicero and Vergil in the sense that he is telling his readers that the means of salvation as Latins understood them are now actually available to those who have accepted the truth about Christ to which Rome has been blinded by its false gods.

Since Tertullian has already claimed to possess a truer understanding of the issues of the present than that of Rome herself, it is not surprising that much of the rest of his time is devoted to attacking the assumption that Roman destiny is in the hands of the pagan deities—that "it is as a reward for their great diligence to their religion that the Romans have been elevated and established in such grandeur that they have become masters of the world, and that these prove to be gods because they flourish more who render them honor" (*Apology* XXV.1). Tertullian attacks this view by observing caustically that many of the Roman deities are foreign in origin and must have betrayed their own worshipers if they are responsible for Rome's rise to power (XXV.2-12). Moreover, viciously taking up Rome's vaunted early simplicity of life, he observes that the triumph of Roman power came at a time when elaborate homage was not paid to the gods, and that in fact the cruel destruction of cities—including their pagan temples—which accompanies any such triumph can scarcely be called piety (XXV.13-17). The truth is, he concludes, that it is not the pagan deities but the true God who determines the destinies of empires:

> See, then, if the dispenser of kingdoms is not that one who is master both of the world which is ruled and of man who rules it. See if the one who controls the rise and fall of empires, and assigns to each its time in the present age, is not the one who was before all time and made the present age a body of times (*corpus temporum*). See if the one who causes states to rise and fall is not the one who ruled over the human race when there were no states (XXVI.1).

Overtones of Justin's association of the true God with the god of philosophy rather than with the gods of popular religion are still felt here, and the reference to God as the ruler of "times" may well be an anticipation of the later Christian use of Stoic notions regarding the interval (Gk: *diastēma*) of time accompanying the moving cosmos. But Tertullian has obviously long since been diverted from Justin's concern with contemporary philosophical issues by his own belief that God is the determiner of the very human happenings which Rome itself regards as providential; and it is notable that the "times" he mentions have become the eras in which one human power after another has been allowed to maintain its rule.

Tertullian proceeds to point out what he conceives to be the implications of God's control of Roman destiny. Accepting the view that Rome is the last of the world empires—a view which Christians had always shared with Rome itself, albeit on somewhat different grounds—he observes that Christians have every reason "to pray for the emperors, and even for the entire imperial establishment and for all things Roman" since they know "that the continuation of the Roman *imperium* restrains the great shock which impends over the whole world, the very end of this age . . ." (XXXII.1). But in any case, it is evident on the face of it that "Caesar is more ours (than yours), since our God established him" (XXXIII.1). The remark about praying for the emperors' welfare in order to forestall the future is a classic instance of Tertullian's irony, since Christians presumably have nothing to fear and much to gain by the "end of this age." The real point is simply that it is Christians rather than pagans who give homage to the true dispenser of Roman prosperity.

This latter point leads Tertullian to his next observation. The calamities presently besetting the empire do not, he insists, reflect the disfavor of the pagan deities with the spread of Christianity. On the contrary, they are divine punishments inflicted by the true God on the empire, which he maintains in existence despite its refusal to recognize him. Here Tertullian goes so far as to assert that human ills have actually moderated since the advent of Christ, "for from that time virtue tempered the wickedness of this age and intercessors with [the true] God appeared" (XL.13). But his main concern is to fix the blame for the calamities of the present on the pagans themselves: "You yourselves, therefore, are the troublers of human affairs, you who always bring on public calamities, by whom God is spurned and the idols worshipped" (XLI.1).

It is particularly important to see that this observation is a jibe at those who hold Christianity responsible for the catastrophes presently besetting Rome. Despite his assertion regarding the recent moderation of human ills, Tertullian holds out no hope that general acceptance of Christianity will forestall the end of the present age. For him as for other Christians of his time, the future course of events had already been revealed in the Scriptures, and the destiny in store for Rome made all too clear. Indeed, while his remarks certainly assume the common Roman notion that worship of the true God will issue in human security and prosperity—what has been called the *do ut des* principle, "I give so that you will give in return"—their poignancy derives from the very fact that he believes that Rome's doom has already been pronounced. Unless this fact is grasped—and here again the peculiar existential purpose of the work sheds light on its contents—we shall fail to understand the sense in which Tertullian unwittingly prepared the way for Latin Christian interpretations of the new relationship between Christianity and the Roman *imperium* which Constantine was to establish.

Before he brings the *Apology* to an end, Tertullian takes occasion to protest the fact that Christians suffer persecution while philosophers, equally skeptical about the pagan deities but less notable for their moral vigor, go unscathed. His protest is of interest no less for its continuation of Justin's identification of the true God with that of the philosophers than for its stress on the significance of moral reform which loomed so large in both his thinking and that of his Latin pagan predecessors. But in fact Tertullian's defense of Christianity has already been set forth in all its essentials before this stage is reached. That defense involves a startling transformation of themes inherited from Greek Christians into an assertion that it is through Christ and not Rome that the issues of the present are to be understood and the power to meet its challenge acquired. His message stands in the tradition of Cicero and Vergil with the one, for him doubtless terrifying, difference that it announces not Rome's continuing grandeur but her inevitable doom.

While the *Apology* states the claims of Christianity in the face of Roman paganism, the shorter treatise *On Prescriptions of Heretics* states those claims in the face of Gnosticism. The latter work, which contrives to summarize the position taken in Tertullian's various polemics against various Gnostic teachers, is as clearly dependent on Irenaeus as was its predecessor on Justin. It is of interest to us both because it provides further evidence of Tertullian's use of Greek Christian ideas and because it addresses itself more directly than the other to the meaning of Christian commitment as such.

Tertullian's work is based on the main themes of Irenaeus' attack on Gnostic claims to possess the apostles' secret teaching. The essence of the apostles' teaching is to be found in the Rule of Faith (XII-XIV). The charge that this Rule, preserved in all the apostolic churches, represents a false version of their message is absurd for the simple reason that it is impossible that "so many churches would have erred into one faith" (XXVIII). Moreover, the Gnostics can show nothing like the evidence of continuity with the apostles' teaching provided by the succession of bishops in the apostolic churches:

> Let them exhibit the origin of their churches, let them unroll the list of their bishops, coming down from the beginning by succession in such a way that their first bishop had for his originator or predecessor one of the apostles or apostolic men (XXXII).

Indeed, the Gnostic teachings were denied apostolic authority from the very first:

> I enter (against them) an examination of the actual teachings which then, in the time of the apostles, were brought to light and rejected by those same apostles. For they will be more easily refuted when they are discovered either to have been already in existence at that time or have taken their seeds from those which then existed (XXXIII).

But Tertullian's divergence from Irenaeus is found in his refusal to allow the kind of dispute over the Gnostic interpretations of the Scriptures which was Irenaeus' major preoccupation. Since the notion that the Gnostics are "the rightful owners of the scriptures" is patently false (XV), he argues, the contents of the Scriptures should not be debated with them:

> It follows that we must not appeal to the scriptures and we must not contend on ground where victory is impossible or uncertain or not certain enough. Even if a dispute over the scriptures did not leave the parties on a par, the natural order of things would demand that one point should be decided first—the point which alone calls for discussion now, namely, who holds the faith to which the scriptures belong, and from whom, through whom, when and to whom was the teaching delivered by which men become Christians (XIX).

This contention is enshrined in the very form of the treatise *On Prescriptions of Heretics,* which offers itself as a series of legal objections (*praescriptiones*) against the claim of a plaintiff being heard.

Tertullian's argument is a kind of *tour de force,* and his own polemics against various Gnostic teachers show no hesitation about disputing their interpretations of the Scriptures. But his point is a serious one. What he has done is to reformulate the arguments by which Irenaeus sought to justify interpreting the Scriptures in the light of the Rule of Faith preserved in the churches into a view of Christianity as the unique introduction among men of the phenomenon of faith in God's message. The fundamental question about the Gnostics thus becomes the one which he states explicitly —whether they hold "the faith to which the scriptures belong" and are those "to whom . . . the teaching . . . by which men become Christians" has been given. Tertullian's denial is based on the evidence already cited. The Gnostics do not acknowledge the Rule of Faith, do not stand in the succession along which it has been passed, and hold views which were at the outset repudiated by the apostles themselves.

But Tertullian has an equally specific view of the nature of Gnosticism. As its teachings show, it involves the very reliance on philosophy rather than faith which Paul warned against in Colossians 2:8 and which he himself encountered during his sojourn in Athens (VII). Moreover, Gnosticism has been introduced into the world in fulfillment of the prophecies regarding the troubling of the elect in the last days "so that those who are approved may be manifest, those who did not stray into heresy as well as those who stood firm in persecution" (IV). Thus the proper reaction—indeed, the reaction which Gnosticism was designed to promote—is one of faith rather than dispute. It is in this connection that Tertullian pronounces his famous dictum:

> What has Jerusalem to do with Athens, the Church with the Academy, the Christian with the heretic? Our principles come from the Stoa of Solomon, who had himself taught that the Lord is to be sought in simplicity of heart. I have no use for a Stoic or a Platonic or a dialectical Christianity. After Jesus Christ we have no need for speculation, after the Gospel no need for research (VII).

Attention has often been called to the inconsistency between this denunciation of Greek philosophy and Tertullian's own frequent use of philosophical ideas, and he himself enunciates elsewhere a more careful—and extremely interesting—view of the dangers of confusing knowledge of the orderly physical cosmos with the revelation of the purposes of God which leaves room for a reasoned faith (e.g., *On the Soul* II). But his famous dictum, hyperbolic though it may be, must be understood in its context as a declaration of the faith which Tertullian believes is required by the issues of the time.

Tertullian's interpretation of Gnosticism is, in its own way, based on Irenaeus' analysis of the philosophical ingredients in the heretical systems which he attacks. But here again, the Irenaean theme is transformed from an important consideration in the criticism of Gnostic views into a clue to the place of Gnosticism in the purposes of God. It is a phenomenon intended to serve the same function as the persecutions—that of providing the circumstances in which true Christians may affirm their faith before the world in its last days. Those familiar with the Latin pagan works of the late Republic and early Empire will immediately identify the similarities between this view and that understanding of the human condition which underlies the claims of Cicero and Vergil to understand the possibilities for self-fulfillment inherent in the circumstances of their time. In effect, Tertullian, who has already asserted in his *Apology* that Christianity possesses the key to the issues of the present which Rome falsely thought to lie in its hands, here interprets the crisis confronting the Church as a challenge to Christians analogous to that which earlier Latin pagans had seen confronting the true Romans of their day. The treatise *On Prescriptions of Heretics* thus not only fills out the picture of Tertullian's Greek Christian inheritance but further reveals the Latin character of his own understanding of the Christian message.

Among the features which set Tertullian's thought off from that of his Greek Christian sources, his quite different approach to the total course of human happenings as part of the course of events with which Christians are concerned is perhaps the most obvious. In fact, the *Apology* claims for Christianity nothing else but a true understanding of the very events with which Latins themselves were preoccupied. Thus his views not only intersect those of the Latin historians but actually involve him in giving his own interpretation of Rome's rise to greatness. The fact to be recognized here is that Tertullian's understanding of the human problem and of God's efforts to deal with it is markedly different from that of his Greek Christian contemporaries. His is the Latin assumption that the real question before men is that of the issues confronting them in the events of their time. His commitment to Christianity is ultimately grounded in his conviction as to the truth of its revelation of the meaning of those events in contrast to the tragic miscalculation of that meaning made by Latin paganism.

At the same time, Tertullian remains as unconcerned with *historia* as are his Greek Christian contemporaries. His understanding of the issues inherent in present events is no less imposed from without, so to speak, than had been those of the philosopher Cicero or the poet Vergil. Moreover, for him in particular, such reflection on the sources of Roman greatness as had been undertaken by the great Roman historians was of little use for the specific reason that he believed that greatness to have nearly run its course. With the final judgment against Rome soon to be pronounced by God, such considerations were of little use.

THE "TERTULLIANISM" OF CYPRIAN

The principal heir of the great Carthaginian theologian, Bishop Caecilius Cyprianus Thascius, fills out our picture of this period chiefly by showing why the attention of Latin Christians in the last century of persecution was directed toward internal Christian matters rather than toward the relations of the Church and the pagan *imperium*.

The divergence between the views of Cyprian and his predecessor results from the fact that the former found himself bishop of the Carthaginian Church at the time of the Novatianist schism, the second outbreak within half a century of the same distrust of laxity in adherence to the faith which had led Tertullian to seek a new source of strength in the Montanist sect. It will probably not seem to us now that the policy of admitting those who had lapsed in the Decian persecution to the status of lifelong, excommunicated penitents—the policy which, in one form or another, was accepted by Pope Cornelius and subsequently agreed to by the Carthaginian Church itself—should be regarded as a sign of laxity on the part of the body of Catholic Christians. Such was, however, the view of the Novatianists, with which Cyprian had to contend at the same time that he met the claim of those released at the end of the persecution to be confessors possessed of divine power to remit the guilt of the lapsed without reference to episcopal authority. It was in these circumstances that Cyprian was compelled to defend his authority in matters of discipline while remaining true to Tertullian's view of Christianity as the introduction into the world of the phenomenon of uncompromising faith in the revelation of God's purposes through Christ. The resulting problems account for most of the pronouncements which come from the brief period of his episcopate—an episcopate which ended in Cyprian's own martyrdom.

Cyprian's debt to Tertullian immediately manifests itself in his treatise *On the Lapsed*. The significance of the persecution, he writes, is that "the Lord has desired his family to be proved; and because a long peace had corrupted the discipline that had been divinely delivered to us, the heavenly rebuke has (thus) aroused our faith, which was giving way" (V). But so far as the lapsed themselves are concerned, they must realize that "the Lord himself alone can have mercy." Moreover, while "the merits of the martyrs and the works of the righteous (i.e., the "confessors") are of great avail with the judge, that will be when the day of judgment shall come, when . . . his people shall stand before the tribunal of Christ" (XVII). The implication is that for the present a penitential preparation for the judgment is alone a realistic policy for the lapsed to pursue.

Like Tertullian, then, Cyprian interprets the events of the

present as designed to provoke that unflinching faith which is the very stuff of Christianity. For him the lapsed, like the Gnostic teachers attacked by Tertullian, have not merely compromised that faith but shown that they do not possess it. They are, in effect, the unfortunate victims of God's efforts to ensure its manifestation. Cyprian's so-called laxness consists ultimately in his refusal to foreclose the possibility of salvation for the lapsed. Apart from its relation to his pastoral office, its origin is traceable to certain interesting reflections of his own, such as those which accompany his unusual description of his own conversion (*Letters* I.3-4), on the impossibility of altering the direction of the will unaided by God. But in all other respects his position rigidly conforms to Tertullian's view of Christianity as a living response to the revelation of Christ called forth by and sustained in the face of the events of the last days.

Cyprian's teaching on the unity of the Church, enunciated in the face of the Novatianist withdrawal from the Catholic body over the questions of the lapsed, has often been taken as a defense of the institutional continuity of Christianity. In fact, it is once again based on a Tertullianist approach to the issues of the time. In his treatise *On the Unity of the Catholic Church*, the origin of the schism is laid to the Devil, who, when he "had been exposed and laid low by the coming of Christ," fabricated heresies and schisms in an effort "to undermine faith, pervert truth, and break unity" (III). The fatal flaw of such movements—and here again one may recall Tertullian's tracing of the alien origins of Gnosticism—is revealed by the fact that they lack that unity which has from the first been seen in such things as the singling out of the one man Peter (Mt. 16:18-19) as a visible embodiment of Christianity and is perpetuated in the solidarity of the episcopate (*Unity* IV-V). Cyprian's stress on the unity of the (true) episcopate is determined, of course, by the consecration of Novatian at Rome and by the presence of a schismatical bishop at Carthage itself. But his ultimate concern is with the reality which that unity reflects; and it is in this connection that, in the course of drawing scriptural proofs of the unique fact of the unity of the Christian body, he combines the themes of the Church as bride (Rev. 21:9) and mother (12:1-6) in his famous statement:

> The bride of Christ cannot be made an adulteress. . . . It is she who keeps us for God and seals for the kingdom the sons she has borne. If you abandon the Church and join yourself to an adulteress, you are cut off from the promises of the Church. . . . You cannot have God for your father unless you have the Church for your mother (VI).

What must be insisted upon here is that, while Cyprian is immediately and even personally involved in defending the maintenance of communion with the true episcopate, his argument proceeds on the assumption that unity must be a living characteristic of the association of men which has sprung out of the revelation given by Christ. Thus unity is, as he later asserts, one of the things demanded for salvation: when the Lord says that "wheresoever two or three are gathered, I . . . am with them (Mt. 18:19-20)," he means that he is "with the single-hearted and peaceable, with those who fear God and keep his commandments" (*Unity* XII). Moreover, the maintenance of unity is, as he says still later, a challenge issued by the times: for "now [schism's] cruel havoc has increased. . . . So it must be at the end of the world, as the Holy Spirit foretells and forewarns through the Apostle: 'In the last days perilous times shall come . . .' (II Tim. 3:1 ff.). Everything that was foretold is being fulfilled. Now it has come, testing men and time alike, as the end of the age draws near" (*Unity* XVI).

Cyprian's position here differs from Tertullian's—that of the Catholic bishop from that of the schismatic presbyter. But it is a difference created by Cyprian's elevation of unity to a special place among the visible manifestations of the Christianity which he, like Tertullian, regards as a conscious response to the events which mark the closing of the present age. It is only when this point is grasped that the continuing Latin Christian quest for a pure Christianity which was yet to produce the most dangerous outbreak of sectarianism, the Donatistic schism of the early fourth century, can be fully appreciated.

It must suffice for the moment, however, to observe that the chief immediate result of Tertullian's work was a discussion of the nature of the response required of Christians by the circumstances of the time rather than further concern for the place of Rome in God's plan. There were, indeed, cross-currents to be observed. Arnobius of Sicca, probably writing in the first years of the new century, prefaced his treatise *Against the Pagans* with a renewed attack on the pagan notion that Christianity was responsible for the calamities of the time. Arguing that there have been fewer calamities since the appearance of Christ, he goes so far as to say that

the world, ungrateful as it is, has long had this benefit from Christ by whom the rage of madness has been softened and has begun to withhold hostile hands from the blood of fellow beings. And if all would . . . lend an ear to his wholesome and peaceful commandments . . . the world . . . would be passing its days in the most placid tranquillity (I.6).

This celebrated passage is based on the same logic as that already encountered in Origen's reply to Celsus concerning pagan charges against Christians, though it should be noted that Arnobius differs from Origen on the important score that he explains the influence of Christ in terms of his effect on the concrete actions of men. In fact, however, Arnobius' statement is no more than a passing observation in the course of what is in style and contents an elaboration of Tertullian's own reply to the views of his opponents.

Recent emphasis on the sporadic character of the persecutions has put in a new light such evidence as we possess of Christian expectations of a possible readjustment of relations with the empire. In particular, the remarks of Arnobius and the early views of Eusebius of Caesarea—with which we shall shortly deal—may be read in this fashion. But the point is that so long as events did not conspire to effect a more drastic change in imperial policy than the mere cessation of persecutions, there was little reason for Christians to question the generally accepted view of Rome's ultimate destiny. Certainly, none of the writers we have considered foresaw the shape of things to come.

THE GOSPEL ON THE EVE OF THE
RECOGNITION OF THE CHURCH

We have thus far pursued our two purposes of investigating the destiny of the Christian message of the action of God in the course of events and its relation to classical *historia* through the Greek and Latin writers of the period of persecution. It will be well, before proceeding further, to restate in more concrete terms some of our earlier observations on the whole subject of the Gospel and history.

Let us, then, return to the point that it is impossible simply to ask whether the writers of the period continued to locate God's actions in "history." The Patristic writers, who knew far more than their predecessors of the New Testament period about *historia*, would never for a moment have thought of locating God's actions in what they knew as an aspect of intellectual endeavor. At the same time, they entered into discussion with the representatives of contemporary pagan culture profoundly convinced of the unique actions of God of which they were witnesses and of the end of the present age which those actions heralded. This fact is nowhere more impressively demonstrated than in the work of Origen, since even his highly speculative interpretations of the Scriptures are far more closely related to the problem of the meaning of God's actions than are the views of many of the modern inheritors of his view of the Scriptures as repositories of divine truth.

The far more important question to ask of these writers is to what extent their discussion with contemporary pagan culture helped or hindered them in their exposition of this central theme of the original preaching. Here it should be clear that the cosmological and anthropological problems confronting the Greek Christians of the period made it increasingly difficult for them to invest a concrete course of events with ultimate significance, while quite the contrary was the case with their Latin Christian contemporaries, confronted as *they* were with a culture which owed its uniqueness precisely to its preoccupation with Rome's rise to world power. Even where the attention of Latin Christians focused on the perplexing question of the inner response which events demanded of Christians, their views reflect a vivid awareness of the reality of those events which is somehow lost to the Greeks. This does not mean, let us hasten to point out, that the Latins had any more objective grasp of some abstract Christian teaching regarding God's action than did the Greek Christians from whom they received the Gospel. Rather, it means that they inherited the message of God's actions in the midst of a culture which had long been given to serious reflection on the eventful character of human existence in circumstances at least as difficult as those through which Israel had suffered.

We may thus come to the events now about to overshadow the Christian world with some notion of their general significance. By the very nature of the Gospel itself, we should be prepared for the fact that the recognition of the Church was a profound shock to the Christian mind. It at once shattered earlier expectations regarding the future course of events and commanded attention as the source of new speculations regarding the unfolding purposes of God. Indeed, none of those with whom we must now deal could admit to themselves how seriously this event undermined expectations which ran back into the earliest Christian period; nor can we quite recapture, at this distance and with our perspectives, the immediate sense of the divine initiation of that event which was everywhere apparent at the time. What should be clear to us is that, while no Christian could be entirely impervious to the shocking character of that event, its effect would be felt most fully in the Latin West. Nor should it be hard to see why Latin Christians would be particularly aware of its wider implications. We shall see that it was in these circumstances that the subject matter hitherto largely the province of *historia* at last became an immediate matter of theological concern.

4

The Problem of "Recognition": Eusebius and His Age

FEW EVENTS of our past have so genuinely bemused modern men as the recognition of the Church—more properly, the *substitution* of Christianity for paganism as the official *cultus* of the Roman empire—by the Emperor Constantine and his successors in and after A.D. 313. For Gibbon and the historians of the Enlightenment, this event seemed to herald the tragic suppression of the tradition of classical humanism to which they believed themselves to be the heirs. For Christians who have witnessed the difficulties besetting the national churches of more recent times, this event seems to have marked a disastrous compromise between the Gospel and the world. Such views do more to testify to a general sense of the importance of this event, however, than they do to illuminate either the event itself or its consequences for us.

Looked at in its own terms, the recognition of the Church presents a quite different aspect from that which it has assumed in such modern foreshortenings of the past. It did not bring classical humanism to its end but merely readjusted the relationship between the two continuing entities of the Church and the pagan civilization into which it had been born. Christian reaction to the event, supposing such generalizations to be possible, was more in the direction of an effort to preserve the exclusiveness of Church life and the uniqueness of the Christian calling than in that of compromise with the world. It is this effort which is visible in the extension of catechetical instruction in the face of growing popularity, in the upsurge of asceticism in the face of increasing security and prestige, even in the maintenance of episcopal doctrinal authority in the face of imperial pressure for the resolution of theological controversies. Indeed, it is precisely this effort which gives the brilliant and strangely unfinished period of the Christian empire its peculiar, and to many its intriguing, character.

The central thing to make clear about the recognition of the Church, viewed on its own terms and not in the perspective of its real or supposed effect on later events, is the problem which the very nature of the event itself posed for the Christian understanding of the purposes of God. We do not know what would have been the outcome of the continuation of the policy of persecution had the Diocletian tetrarchy not been overthrown by Constantine and Licinius. Nor do we know what would have been the result of the policy of toleration which the latter apparently preferred. We do know that the policy which Constantine pursued with increasing vigor after his assumption of sole rule in A.D. 324, and which was even more thoroughly articulated by later dynasties, was one which unequivocally committed the *imperium* to the notion that the Christian God and not the pagan deities was the dispenser of Roman fortunes. As we now look back on it, this was the only result other than extinction which Christians could reasonably have expected from their preaching, since neither the ancient Near East—including Israel—nor the classical world offered any precedent for a political power shirking its responsibility to seek aid from such heavenly powers as seemed able to offer it. The notion of a political power religiously neutral is one of the unique results of the circumstances in which modern Western society emerged from the ruins of medieval Christendom.

The problem was that, while Christians had never in principle denied the contention that aid was available to the political power which worshiped the true God, they had in actuality asserted that judgment had virtually already been pronounced against Rome for its congenital inability to recognize that God. Indeed, the inevitable doom of the last of the world empires was a notion which Christianity had inherited from Judaism at the very beginning of its life. It was an assumption of most Christian speculation about the future unfolding of God's purposes, a major source of the confidence with which martyrs and confessors had faced their persecutors, and the background against which the references of Tertullian to the now foreclosed possibilities of further Roman greatness must be set.

The profound inner shock which recognition thus administered to Latin Christians in particular was nothing in comparison with what awaited them when the result of the change of imperial policy was not a renewal of peace and security but a continuation of present disasters—a continuation which lost none of its effect from the fact that neither they nor their pagan critics could foresee that it heralded an end of the *imperium* itself before the end of the present age. But if we are to appreciate that further shock, we must first examine the views of those who sought to come to terms with the immediate event of the recognition of the Church itself. It is noteworthy that their views, as well as those of their successors, are still commonly studied as contributions to the discussion of the relation of Church and State as medieval and modern men have recently come to deal with it. But it should not be hard to see why it can be said that their views constitute a serious effort to reinterpret the purposes of God manifest in the unfolding course of events to which Christians were witnesses.

EUSEBIUS OF CAESAREA

Much of the new light shed on the work of those now commonly called "Eusebians" or "imperial theologians" has come as a result of the re-evaluation of the peculiar figure of Eusebius, bishop of Palestinian Caesarea in the reign of Constantine. A disciple of Pamphilius, student and successor of Origen at Caesarea, Eusebius has chiefly been studied for his uncertain grasp of the

implications of Origen's teaching regarding the "perpetual generation" of the Word and the ambiguous position into which he was
consequently led in the early phase of the Arian or Trinitarian controversy. What is now becoming clear is that, as an interpreter of
the work of Constantine as effecting the merger of Church and
empire into a single society destined to survive to the end of the
present age, he is a far more significant and interesting figure than
has often been imagined.

The work which gained Eusebius the sobriquet "church historian," the ten books of *Ecclesiastical History,* is the first serious
attempt to employ the discipline of *historia* in the recording of
Christian events. As might be expected in a person for whom the
work of the Alexandrian theologians had an appeal, Eusebius
shows himself familiar with the historical approach as he understood it when he declares it his purpose to investigate "the succes-
sions from the holy apostles, together with the times (*chronois*)
which have elapsed since the Savior's day down to our own, together with the important affairs which are said to have been trans-
acted according to the account of the Church (*kata tēn ecclēsistis-
tikōn historian*), and those who took a prominent place as leaders
or presidents in such communities as were especially famous
. . . ," adding "yet my starting point shall be none other than the
beginning of the dispensation of Jesus, our Savior and Lord, the
Christ of God" (*History* I.1.1-2). That is, his purpose remains that
of setting down the things that have happened even though he
feels compelled to place them within a wider theological context—
or to put it another way, he does not feel it his duty to merge his
recording of events with his theology. It has rightly been pointed
out that Eusebius' episodic work, with its tendency to follow the
policy of Josephus in preserving records even when they do not
serve any immediate historical purpose, reflects a certain overarching interest in those records for their own sake which is not found in
comparable Greek pagan writings. Nor is Eusebius' work free from
the normal reflections of a writer's interests and prejudices, as the
apologetic treatment of Origen in Book VI shows very clearly. But

it is still true that the chief value of the work is to be found in its largely nontheological handling of its material. Indeed, it was through Eusebius' influence on successors such as Jerome, Theodoret of Cyrrhus, and Socrates the Historian, who later sought to extend his enterprise to the events of their own time, that the heritage of Greek *historia* passed into later hands.

This does not mean that the *Ecclesiastical History* is unimportant for the study of Eusebius' view of the recognition of the Church. Indeed, it provides us with our best picture of both its sources and its development. While disagreement still exists with respect to the precise stages of the preparation of the work as a whole, it is generally recognized that the first nine books took shape in the light of a policy of toleration such as that favored by Licinius rather than of the later policy of Constantine. Its initial statement of its intention to carry its account to the "martyrdoms that took place in our own day, and the gracious and kindly succor of our Savior at the end of all" (I.1.2) is consistent with its closing reference to the action of Constantine and Licinius "to purge the world of enmity against God, conscious of the good things which he had bestowed upon them" (IX.11.9), though even the latter may be a substitute for an original reference to the bestowal on the Church of "peace from troubles without and troubles in the heart" (*ibid.*, var.). Though it is not explicitly stated in this work, Eusebius' view of the significance of these happenings is that suggested by the lengthy quotation which he gives from the letter of Melito of Sardis to the Emperor Antoninus Pius, where it is asserted that it is important for the emperor to "safeguard that philosophy (*i.e.*, Christianity) which grew up with the empire and took its start under Augustus," for "since the principate of Augustus no misfortune has befallen [the empire]; on the contrary all things have been splendid and glorious" (IV.26.7-8). Eusebius himself espoused much the same view when he wrote in his *Preparation for the Gospel* that "immediately after Augustus had established his sole rule, at the time of our Savior's appearance, the rule of the multitude was abolished among the Romans. And from that time to the present you cannot see, as before, cities at war with cities, nor nation fighting with nation, nor life being worn away in the confusion of everything" (I.4). There is no question that he generally foresaw the establishment of toleration as heralding the end of an unnatural conflict between Christianity and the empire, and the establishment of an era of peace and security for both. His view is that which we have noted in Origen among the Greek and Arnobius among the Latin writers of the era of persecution, with the one crucial difference that what they saw as only an abstract possibility has been transformed for him into an actuality by the events of his own time.

The tenth book of the *Ecclesiastical History* contains a brief account of the joint rule of Constantine and Licinius, their eventual conflict, and the assumption of sole rule by Constantine. Its main purpose, however, is to serve not merely as an extension of the account of the earlier books but as a means of bringing them into line with what Eusebius now regarded as the true significance of the events which he had recorded in them. What those events heralded, he now declared, was nothing else than the perfection of the Augustan empire at the hands of the Christian emperor:

> Constantine, the mighty victor, resplendent with every virtue that godliness bestows . . . formed the Roman Empire, as in days of old, into a single united whole. . . . There was taken away from men all fear of those who formerly oppressed them. . . . Thus truly, when all tyranny had been purged away, the kingdom that belonged to them was preserved stedfast and undisputed for Constantine and his sons; who, when they had made it their first action to cleanse the world from hatred of God, conscious of the good things he had bestowed upon them, displayed their love of virtue and of God, their pride and gratitude toward the deity, by their manifest deeds in the sight of men (X.9.6-9).

What Eusebius has here done, by establishing a correspondence between the sole rule of Augustus and Constantine, is to convert the Augustan principate into a virtual foreshadowing of the establishment of the Constantinian dynasty. Through the help of the *Ecclesiastical History*, then, we can actually watch the emergence of Eusebius' view of the work of Constantine as being not merely the end of an unnatural conflict between Christianity and the empire, but the achievement of a new stage in the perfection of human life.

The full development of Eusebius' view is found in works of a very different character from the Christian *historia*. Indeed, the later works show several different tendencies which, while obviously closely related, are never fully combined into a single whole. The first tendency is that found in the oration *In Praise of Constantine*, where Eusebius comments in daring fashion on the theological significance of Constantine as that of exercising a rule over the physical creation subordinate but similar to that of the divine Word himself over the entire cosmos. The one who is God's "priorly-existing and unique Word . . . older than all time and every age (*pantos chronou kai pantōn aiōnōn*) . . . holds a supreme dominion over the whole cosmos . . . , from whom and by whom our emperor, beloved of God, bearing a kind of image (*eikona*) of the supreme rule as it were in imitation (*kata mimēsin*) of the greater, directs the course of all things upon earth" (I.6). The function of the emperor, Eusebius pursues, is to subdue, to discipline, and to direct by his virtuous example within his particular sphere those over whom he has been set by God (II.1-4) as one who exercises over the body the dominion which the Word exercises over the soul (VII.1-2, 5-7). While Eusebius' precise views on the question of the "perpetual generation" of the Word seem to have remained fairly obscure even to Eusebius himself, there is no denying that this line of argument employs just those themes of subordination and merited authority which the early Arians derived from Origen and which he employed in constructing his picture of the status of the Christian emperor in the divine plan for the perfection of the creation.

A second tendency is that found in the *Commentary on the Psalms* and the *Commentary on Isaiah*, in which various of the prophecies of an earthly fulfillment of Israel's hopes hitherto generally applied by Christians to the life of the coming kingdom of God are taken to refer to what he calls a divine *politeia* or *politeuma*, a perfect ordering of the physical creation which will only be superseded by the final restoration of souls to God. Notable here is the reversal of the interpretation of the earthly Jerusalem as a foreshadowing of the heavenly city to come at the end of the age (Gal. 5:25-6; Rev. 21:10-22:5; cf. Origen, *Principles* IV.3.8-9), which occurs in his references to both the Church and the divine *politeia* as a present image of the heavenly city (Ps. 96:2-4; 50:21; Isa. 22:1; 49:11; 54:6-10). Eusebius is rather unclear as to the precise meaning of his divine *politeia*, but there is no question that he has in mind a Christian commonwealth larger than the Church as formerly constituted if not in all respects the literal equivalent of the dominion of the Christian emperor. Indeed, he is of necessity unclear, since he is announcing the arrival of a stage of the perfection of the creation which seems to him indicated by present events but inevitably eludes identification with the immediate circumstances of human existence.

Recent interest in Eusebius' views has not been misplaced. At the same time, those views need to be considered carefully in the light of his place in the broader currents of thought in the time. It must not be overlooked that his sympathy with the early Arians is first of all a witness to his place among those of his contemporaries particularly influenced by Origen. All that he says about the person of the Christian emperor and the perfection of the physical creation which his work has inaugurated must be read in the light of the assumption that salvation has fundamentally to do with the establishment of communion between souls and the divine Word, and with *its* perfection at the restoration of all things. Whatever Eusebius thought of the place of the physical creation in the divine purpose—and, as co-author with Pamphilius of the *Apology for Origen*, he is chiefly on record simply as denying the importance of Origen's speculations in this regard—he did not ultimately think very highly of the heritage to which Constantine had succeeded.

More generally, however, it must be recognized that Eusebius had few disciples among his Greek Christian successors. The important tradition of Christian *historia* which he helped to establish was perpetuated without reference to his views regarding the recognition of the Church. The immediate future, as the work of Athanasius and the Cappadocian Fathers shows only too well, was dominated by the cosmological and anthropological problems bequeathed to Greek Christians by the Alexandrians. It was not until the time of Justinian, more than two centuries later, that a remnant of the Constantinian empire was to be justified in its increasingly isolated position in world affairs as the means by which the physical creation was formed into an "image" of the heavenly world in the manner of the theologies of Maximus the Confessor and Pseudo-Dionysius.

But Eusebius is nevertheless important. His unfinished views —and they are, at some points, sketchy to say the least—are evidence of the arresting character of the events of the time and of the optimism which they aroused in the Christians who witnessed them. The very fact that neither his understanding of the practice of *historia* nor his Origenist theological heritage afforded him much precedent for his announcement of the formation of the divine *politeia* in the work of Constantine contributes to the picture which he gives us of a person forced under the pressure of unanticipated happenings to speak to the issues which they raised.

THE IMPERIAL THEOLOGY IN THE LATIN WEST

The Latin Christian fourth century was no less creative and complicated than the Greek. It was the century which witnessed both the last and most dangerous outbreak of Latin sectarianism in the Donatist schism and the increasing involvement of Latin Christians in the Arian or Trinitarian controversy. It was the century in which the theological heritage of Tertullian continued to make its influence felt at the same time that such cosmopolitan figures as Ambrose, Jerome, and Augustine were becoming aware of the sophisticated theological issues being debated by Greek Christians in the aftermath of the work of the Alexandrian School of Clement and Origen.

It will come as no surprise, however, that the impact of the recognition of the Church is far more evident in the writings of the Latin Christians of the century than in those of their Greek Christian contemporaries. The notion that the true God would confer blessings on his worshipers stood in their past as no residual idea or general proposition. The *do ut des* ("I give so that you will give in return") was no less part of the Latin pagan interpretation of Rome's rise to greatness than of the Latin Christian understanding of the Gospel as the true interpretation of the total course of human happenings. Moreover, the grounds on which Tertullian had defended the Gospel were such as to affirm the truth of *do ut des* in the same breath that it declared it forever inapplicable in the case of Rome. The events which Eusebius witnessed were such as to administer a greater shock and to suggest rather different implications to the Latin Christians of the time. Indeed, it is misleading to speak of the views of his contemporaries as "Eusebian" in any specific sense, since they were the spontaneous and independent efforts of people far more sensitive than he to the same events which engaged his attention.

LACTANTIUS

The immediate Latin Christian response to the new religious policy of the empire was that of Lucius Caecilius Firmianus Lactantius. Probably a student of Arnobius (cf. Jerome, *On Illustrious Men* LXXX), the author of writings more extensive than profound, Lactantius had once enjoyed the patronage of the Emperor Diocletian in the capacity of a teacher of Latin rhetoric. In his old age he was appointed by Constantine, in A.D. 317, to be the tutor of his son Crispus. His career thus parallels that of Eusebius in a number of ways, though he apparently had no contact with his Greek contemporary. His authorship of the grisly treatise *On the Deaths of the Persecutors*, with which we are here concerned, is now generally accepted, though its authorship is not a matter which directly concerns us. The work unquestionably dates from the pe-

riod of the joint rule of Constantine and Licinius and is concerned
to make clear the issues now facing men in the wake of their reversal of the religious policy of the Diocletian tetrarchy.

In his earlier *Divine Institutes,* written in the midst of the
Diocletian persecution, Lactantius had addressed pagan readers regarding the end of the present age in terms which virtually repro-
duced the themes of Tertullian. There is no question, he wrote,
that "the fall and ruin of the world will shortly take place, although
it seems that nothing of that kind is to be feared so long as Rome
remains intact," adding sardonically that, so far as Christians are
concerned, God is "to be entreated by us and implored—if indeed
his laws and decrees can be delayed—lest sooner than we think
[Anti-Christ] should come" (VII.25.6-8). In the present work, however, he begins on the quite different note that a new future may be
expected from the reversal of policy which has occurred under Constantine and Licinius:

> Behold, all the adversaries are destroyed, and tranquillity has been re-
> established throughout the Roman Empire, the recently oppressed Church
> rises again, and the temple of God, overthrown by the hands of the wicked,
> is built more glorious than before. For God has raised up princes to rescind
> the impious and sanguinary edicts of the tyrants and to provide for the well-
> being of mankind, so that now the cloud of times past is dispelled and peace
> and serenity gladdens the heart (*On the Deaths of the Persecutors* I).

This new note may well seem at first sight to contradict the others.
On reflection, however, it is a response to the extraordinary events of
the time, similar in character to the Tertullianist themes which it
supplants. It is a response quite different from the reasonable approach of Eusebius, since it proceeds from a more vivid impression
of the intervention of God in the events of the present and is less
concerned with the ultimate significance of that intervention in the
totality of God's dealings with his creatures.

The purpose of the work quickly appears. The happiness of
the time must not be allowed to obscure the lessons which recent
events have to teach. The punishments inflicted on the persecuting
emperors were intended by God to show "by great and marvelous

examples . . . that he alone is God, and that with fit vengeance he executes judgment on the proud, the impious, and the persecutors" (*ibid.*). His purpose is thus similar to that of his Latin predecessors, as it is unlike that of his Greek contemporary. It is to record the evidence of God's concrete judgment on the opponents of the Church—and to do so, of course, that those who follow may grasp the issues which face them in their actions.

We need not delay over the body of the work. It is an appalling account of the pride, avarice, and lust uniformly characteristic of those emperors who had taken special delight in the recent persecutions, as well as of the means adopted by God to visit their people with disaster and themselves with dishonor, defeat, and death. There can scarcely be any work, pagan or Christian, more typically Latin in its grim insistence on pointing the lessons of the time rather than conforming to the spirit of the occasion. It is more important, however, to note the terms in which Lactantius finally restates his purpose as being "to commit [these things] to writing exactly as they happened, lest the memory of events so important should perish, or lest someone who should wish to write an account (*historiam*) should corrupt the truth" (LII). The work immediately concludes with a call to Christians to pray that God will "confirm throughout the age the peace which . . . he has bestowed," but his real purpose once again is to alert those responsible for the general welfare with what is in store for them should they themselves disturb that peace.

The treatise *On the Deaths of the Persecutors* is a thoroughly unpleasant work. But it is a useful witness to the independence which from the first marked the Latin Christian reaction to the recognition of the Church. In contrast to Eusebius, it takes the assumption that God will bestow his blessings on an empire which no longer thwarts his purposes, not as the basis on which to proclaim the inauguration of a new society but as reason for clarifying the issues now set before those who must act in the time ahead. Moreover, the work attempts no proof of the theological importance of the achievement of Constantine but proceeds from an interpretation of recent events as immediate evidence of God's providential control of human happenings. In the latter connection it is to be noted that it offers itself as a true account of events which no future historian must be allowed to obscure. Lactantius does not write as a historian, though the similarities between his treatment of the Diocletian tetrarchy and Tacitus' catalogue of the corruptions of the Julian House are too obvious to be missed. Nevertheless, his approach is one which broadly parallels the search of great Latin historians for the clue to the course of Roman affairs—the very point at which their work differs from that of the Greek practitioners of *historia* with whom Eusebius was familiar. We have this tendency already in the work of Tertullian. The difference here is that Lactantius' approach leads him to offer an independent interpretation of the past and forecast of the future which he thinks can and will be borne out by reference to specific happenings in Roman political affairs. We shall soon see that this was to prove to be dangerous ground to occupy.

AMBROSE OF MILAN

Lactantius did not live to see the assumption of sole rule by Constantine, and we do not know what his reaction would finally have been to the fully developed policies in the light of which Eusebius' mature views were stated. Any fear that his views would have drastically altered in the circumstances can be at once allayed by reference to the attitude displayed toward Christian emperors at the end of the century by Ambrose, Bishop of Milan, the city which had become the administrative center of the West after the removal of the imperial capital to Constantinople. That attitude is one which sees Christian emperors simply as laymen called to a special responsibility for the welfare of their people and under a special obligation to accept the pronouncements of the bishop regarding the actions required in the fulfillment of that responsibility.

A classic instance of Ambrose's implementation of his views

is found in his letter to the young Valentinian II concerning the request of certain pagan senators for the maintenance of the Altar of Victory in the Senate House at Rome (*Letter* XVII). The very first words of the letter state unequivocally that the issue before the emperor is one which bears directly on the future welfare of the empire:

> As all who live under the sway of Rome serve you, . . . so you serve Almighty God. . . . There can be no other assurance of prosperity than the universal and sincere worship of the true God. . . . Therefore, sir, seeing that from a Christian Emperor God demands not faith alone but zeal and care and devotion, . . . I wonder how some have come to hope that you . . . may order the restoration of heathen altars (1-3).

Nor does Ambrose omit to say what the consequences to the emperor himself will be in the event that he accedes to the pagan request:

> If anything else is decided, we bishops can certainly not accept it with equanimity. . . . You may come to church as you please, but you will find no bishop there, or else one who will resist you. How will you answer a bishop who says to you, "The Church does not want your offerings. The altar of Christ rejects your gifts, for you have made an altar to idols. . . . We cannot associate ourselves with another man's sin." How will you answer to these words? . . . Childhood in faith is no excuse. Even children have confessed Christ fearlessly before their persecutors (13-15).

In fact, Ambrose here interprets the issues facing the Christian emperor in the same terms which Lactantius employs in dealing with his pagan predecessors. Since acknowledgment of the true God is the source of imperial prosperity, there can be no question of the responsibility of the one holding the imperial office. Nor can there, on Ambrose's own view, be any question of the bishop's obligation to see that that responsibility is accepted by one who is first and foremost a Christian.

Even more striking instances of Ambrose's dealings with Christian emperors are found in his correspondence with Theodosius the Great, who was in no small part responsible for the triumph of Nicene orthodoxy at the Council of Constantinople in A.D. 381, as well as being hailed as the author of restrictions against both Arian Christians and pagans. In successive encounters with Theodosius,

Ambrose not only saw fit to interpret Theodosius' demand that Christians accept financial responsibility for the destruction of the Jewish synagogue at Callinicum along the same lines as he had interpreted the case of the Altar of Victory (*Letter* XL), but actually withheld communion from Theodosius until he had done penance for retaliatory measures taken in the case of a riot against the imperial garrison at Thessalonica (*Letter* LI). In each case, Ambrose treated the august person generally recognized in his own day as the savior of Catholic Christianity simply as a holder of imperial office who was also a Christian under episcopal discipline.

The most interesting of the documents to come from the reign of Theodosius, however, is Ambrose's funeral oration *On the Death of Theodosius,* and that for the special reason that he is here no less bent on extolling an emperor's accomplishments than was Eusebius in his account of the greatness of Constantine. Ambrose's praise of Theodosius could scarcely be more different. What engages his attention as he notes Theodosius' edicts against pagan worship (4), his mitigation of the grain tax (5), his trust that God would bring victory to the imperial arms in battle (7), and his numerous acts of mercy (12) is not his unique achievements but his efforts to acquire the virtue for which all Christians must strive. This is nowhere clearer than in the peroration, where Ambrose issues the traditional call to emulate the dead:

> He is victorious who hopes for the grace of God, not he who presumes on his own strength. For why do you not rely on grace, since you have a merciful judge in the contest. . . . Good, therefore, is humility. It delivers those who are in danger and raises those who have fallen. And so, because Theodosius, the emperor, showed himself humble, and, when sin had stolen upon him, asked for pardon, his soul is turned to its rest (25-28).

Ambrose here has in mind the excommunication of Theodosius, for him doubtless the most trying event of their relationship. But his point is a more general one. The greatness of Theodosius *as emperor,* he says, lay in his willingness to acknowledge his dependence on God. In effect, it is for withstanding the temptations of the imperial office that his life is to be celebrated as an example to all Christians.

It is tempting to examine other aspects of Ambrose's understanding of the recognition of the Church, in particular his reply to Symmachus, the spokesman of the pagan senators in the case of the Altar of Victory, that Rome herself has come to maturity by recognizing the true author of her greatness (*Letter* LVIII.7, 23). But our purpose is the more restricted one of employing Ambrose's relations to the Christian emperors of his day to fill out our picture of the Latin Christian reaction to the events which had arrested the attention of Eusebius. For this purpose Ambrose is particularly useful for the reason that he was far better acquainted than Lactantius with the very trends of Greek Christian thought which flowed from the work of the Alexandrian School to that of the contemporary Cappadocian fathers.

But while Ambrose thus stands closer to the very theological tradition from which Eusebius came than did his Latin predecessors, his own views remain fundamentally uninfluenced not only by the daring theological interpretations of the person of Constantine set forth by Eusebius but even by the subtler Greek Christian views of God's attempts to bring the cosmos to perfection on which they are based. For him no less than for Lactantius it is the issues now confronting men as a result of Rome's providential recognition of the true source of its greatness which are the center of attention. In the circumstances in which he found himself, he was thus forced to call such imperial personages as Valentinian II and Theodosius the Great to their responsibilities as Christians charged with the welfare of the Empire. Indeed, it is interesting to note that if Lactantius' treatment of the persecuting emperors is reminiscent of Tacitus' account of the Julian House, Ambrose's conception of the imperial office points back behind the developments which had finally led the Diocletian tetrarchy to introduce the theme of divine kingship common in the ancient Near East and the Hellenistic world. It is virtually a Christian version of the early Augustan interpretations of the imperial office as the central place where the challenge which events have thrust upon Rome must be met. Nor is this the last time that we shall find echoes in Latin Christian writings of the themes of introspection and self-criticism characteristic of the classic period of pagan Latin culture.

PRUDENTIUS

Perhaps the most comprehensive expression of the Latin Christian reaction to the recognition of the Church, and the least familiar, is that of Ambrose's younger contemporary, the Christian poet Aurelius Prudentius Clemens. Prudentius' views are set forth in his refutation in verse of Symmachus' plea for the maintenance of the Altar of Victory, and are found in the two books of his *Against Symmachus*. The immediate occasion of the work is not entirely clear. But since the *relatio* of the learned pagan senator had become a document of importance for those who sought to defend paganism as an integral part of the aesthetic treasures of the classical civilization, it is easy to see how it could become a bone of contention for one who was himself deeply committed to rescuing pagan poetical forms for Christian use.

The first part of Prudentius' work is, indeed, a general attack on the modest pagan intellectual revival in which Symmachus figured rather than on the *relatio* itself. Its main contention is that worship of the pagan deities had all along been a blot on Rome rather than the clue to her greatness—a blot now happily removed, in particular by Theodosius' edicts against continuing paganism:

> I believed that [Rome], once sick with pagan vice
> Had purged herself by now of old disease
> And that no trace remained since our good prince
> Had eased her grievous pains by healing laws.
> But since the plague, of late revived, torments
> The sons of Romulus, we must beg God's help,
> Lest Rome now fall into the ancient mire,
> And togas white be stained again with smoke and blood.
> *Against Symmachus* I.1-8

It was merely from false prudence that the pagan emperors, he continues, had been led to maintain pagan worship. In fact, however, the Christian emperors have been led by their true understanding of the issues facing Rome to take steps that will achieve the prosperity their predecessors sought:

> The remedy of tyrants heretofore
> Has been to see what measures would fulfill
> The present needs, with no concern beyond.
> Alas, how ill they served this people, how
> Ill its fathers [the senate?] too, whom they allowed
> To sink to Tartarus with Jove and all his host.
> But this man has extended his *imperium* to future times
> By striving to assure the commonwealth . . .
> . . . Rome thrives,
> For justice reigns: obey the one who holds
> The power. He commands you to shake off
> The superstitious errors of the past,
> To know no God but him who rules all things
> And shaped the vast dimensions of the world.
>
> *Against Symmachus* I.21-41

Here Prudentius applies to Theodosius' extension of Constantine's policy the Tertullianist logic already released from its earlier confinement by Lactantius. The perpetuation of paganism was not merely blind but wicked. It is only under the Christian dispensation that Rome can expect to live in prosperity because it has at last its responsibility to obey the true God.

In the second part of the work, Prudentius directly attacks Symmachus' view that pagan worship is not only an indifferent matter with educated men but in fact so deeply embedded in the classical past as to be essential to the continuation of human cultural development. On the contrary, he argues, the truth is that the abandonment of paganism is a logical result of that development.

> Why do you speak to me, Roman senator,
> Of ancient rites, when a change of mind
> Has come upon the fathers and the people too?
> Now when it profits us to lay aside
> The manners of the past for newer ways,

> We take delight in the discovery
> Of things not known before; the life of man
> Grows and improves by long experience.
> Such changes may be seen in human life,
> Which varies with each age: the infant crawls,
> The boy totters both in step and mind.
> The robust youth with fiery passion burns.
> Then comes the time of ripe maturity,
> And last, old age, sagacious but infirm,
> Falters in body, but is sound in mind.
>   *Against Symmachus* II.309-323

The passage is one of Prudentius' best efforts, since it offers a peculiarly effective combination of the theme of the ages of man not
infrequently used in the Christian Platonic tradition to describe the
progressive release of the rational soul from the physical passions
(e.g., Methodius, *Symposium* V.2-3) with the theme of the nearing
end of the present age so characteristic of Latin Christian writers.
Rome's true greatness, he says in effect, has been achieved, not in
the establishment of perpetual rule but in its discovery of the true
author of man's ultimate destiny.

But Prudentius is later even more explicit as to the perspective
in which recent events place Rome's progress to maturity, especially
as regards the awesome rule of Augustus. In speaking of the Civil
Wars he writes:

> The public fate or genius or spirit passed
> Through such rude storms; right rule it learned at last,
> And on Augustus' head it placed the diadem. . . .
> If through so many steps and varied schemes
> It formed a rule which still commands respect
> And public loyalty, why does it fear
> To recognize divine authority,
> Unknown before and only now revealed?
> Let us rejoice that Rome, now thrall to Christ,
> Serves God and hates her former cults.
>   *Against Symmachus* II.428-441

This argument is a version of the Christian interpretation of the
work of Augustus which we have already met in the work of Arno-

bius among Latin writers of the era of persecution and which forms the basis on which Eusebius built his view of Constantine. But Prudentius' use of the theme is markedly different from that of Eusebius. The sole rule of the Christian emperor—in this case, of course, that of Theodosius rather than Constantine—is given significance by being set in the context of the concrete events of the Roman past. Moreover, the analogy between Augustus and Theodosius is employed, not to define any special status for the Christian emperor but to assert the immediate importance of the acknowledgment of God's ultimate rule which forms the basis of the issues now confronting Christian Rome in its treatment of resurgent paganism. Indeed, Prudentius' poem develops much the same view of the times as witnessing Rome's achievement of maturity which Ambrose advanced in his reply to Symmachus' *relatio*. His view of the Christian emperor differs from that of his predecessor chiefly in that he now simply claims for Theodosius the position of one who conceded God's ultimate rule, which Ambrose had sought to force the great emperor to accept in his lifetime and praised him for acknowledging after he was dead. For Prudentius, then, the sole rule of the Christian emperor is no less important than it is for Eusebius. But for him it is important not as inaugurating a divine *politeia* in which the perfection of the physical creation is achieved insofar as possible, but as a witness to the fact that Rome's true greatness has finally been achieved in its last days with the acknowledgment of the one whose supreme greatness is reflected in its own past.

It is not unfair to think of Prudentius as the Christian equivalent of the Augustan poets Horace and Vergil, since he confronted his time with a message about a Christian Augustus who had discerned the challenge of the unfolding course of events and had met it on Rome's behalf. Indeed, his own literary gifts are not by any means to be despised, and the freshness of his use of inherited forms reflects the force of his message no less than that of his predecessors'. What has buried him as deeply in the past as the pagans he sought to emulate is that his optimism proved no less premature.

His death in A.D. 405 occurred five years before the sack of Rome by the Gothic troops of Alaric cast in doubt the interpretation which he and his contemporaries had placed upon the recognition of the Church.

SOME GENERAL REMARKS ON THE PROBLEM OF "RECOGNITION"

The assumption that peace and prosperity would be given a people who turned for help to the true God was deeply lodged in the inheritance of fourth-century Christians. It was inherent in both the scriptural and the pagan past, as well as having appeared in various forms in writings of the period of persecution. The views of Eusebius and the Latin imperial theologians, however, embody something more than the application of that assumption to the future of the once hostile Roman *imperium*. Theirs is an interpretation of the policies of Constantine and his successors which sees them as acts of a divine providence which has all along determined that a final era of peace and security should occur before the end of the present age. The Greek Eusebius and his Latin contemporaries express their views in different ways. Eusebius' divine *politeia* is less closely related to his understanding of salvation than its Latin counterparts. On the other hand, the Latins remain vague and even perhaps uncertain as to the place of the present turn of events in the larger scheme of God's purposes at the same time that they are clearer as to the immediate responsibilities which it thrusts upon those charged with Rome's welfare. But for each the events of the time appeared as a revelation of God's purposes far more revolutionary than they could admit even to themselves.

We can now see very easily how naïve was the reliance of these fourth-century Christians on the assumption that the events of the time heralded a period of peace and prosperity. It is harder but more important to recognize their views as an authentic continuation of the logic of the original Christian proclamation of the unfolding course of events as a manifestation of God's purposes. In fact, it is not fanciful to say that it was in their work that Christians at last found themselves facing the same problem of the meaning of human events which Israel had faced as its faith took shape in the midst of the political realities of the ancient Near East. Their ultimate contribution to the development of Christian thought lay in the fact that they recognized and tried to deal, however prematurely, with the implications of the enmeshment of Christianity's fortunes with those of the Roman *imperium* to which they were witnesses.

The providential interpretation of the recognition of the Church launched by fourth-century Christians went to a large extent unchallenged by the representatives of continuing paganism. Symmachus' *relatio*, though it was important enough for Prudentius to attack, was perhaps understandably diplomatic in the restraint with which it limited itself to the insistence that religious matters were less imporant than Christians assumed. But even the books *Against the Galileans*, attributed to the apostate Emperor Julian, the nephew of Constantine who was the last hope of paganism in its search for a further reversal of imperial religious policy, do little more than elaborate Celsus' earlier view that an accurate account of the origins of Christianity provides no reason for thinking that Christians are in touch with the power which controls human destiny. In fact, so long as events themselves did not seriously challenge the interpretation which Christians tended to place upon the events of the time, continuing paganism had little chance of a hearing.

The situation was very different, however, after the sack of Rome in A.D. 410. It was apparently only with this event that the disastrous implications of the catastrophes which had already begun with the resettlement of the semicivilized barbarian tribes within the imperial frontiers began to be recognized. In any case, it was not until this point that Christians—and, in particular, the Latin Christians who had committed themselves in such a specific way to the meaning of present events—realized something of the challenge which lay before them. Nor was it merely a renewal of pagan charges that Christians had betrayed the *imperium* which stung them in the wake of the sack of Rome. What they could not now fail to see was that the truth of Christianity was in jeopardy unless they could find an explanation of the events of the time different from but as comprehensive as that of their too optimistic predecessors.

Before we pass to the successors of the imperialists, however, we must note how they prepared the way for the elevation of the stuff of *historia* to a matter of theological significance. Quite apart from the technical influence of Eusebius' work, the claims of the Latin imperialists were such as to confront their successors with the necessity of resolving the problem thrust upon them in the light of the full course of events which had led to the circumstances now confronting the *imperium*. In fact, no resolution of this problem could be imagined which was not as much historical as theological in character. This is not to say that Christians were to confront a lively opposition from pagan *historia* as such. Indeed, pagan *historia* was now virtually dead. Its last true representative was yet to appear in the impressive sixth-century figure of Ammianus Marcellinus, whose account of the Constantinian and Valentinian dynasties united a concern for the personalities of the emperors reminiscent of Tacitus with a circumspection which harked back to an even earlier time. But Ammianus' adherence to historical principles keeps him from entering the lists against the Christians, except perhaps indirectly in his evident admiration for the Apostate Julian (*History* XXII.1-XV.5). The real debate which was now to take place was within Christian theological circles themselves, where a new concern with the meaning of events was now evident. It is not too much to say that this concern marked a last phase of the classical historical enterprise under Christian auspices.

5

The Crisis of the Christian Empire, I: Augustine

IT IS ONE of the real ironies of the past that the blows which were already beginning to fall on the Christian empire with the so-called barbarian invasions at the end of the fourth century fell most heavily just where their theological effect was likely to be the greatest—the Latin West. The diversion of the semicivilized Arian Christian tribes from the doorstep of the new imperial capital at Constantinople and their resettlement in the less densely populated and less strategically important West ranks with the best of those improvisations which had characterized Rome's rise to world domination. It secured the resources and gained the time needed for the empire to reorganize itself behind its new bastion in the Greek East. But it also confronted the Latin Christians, who had most at stake in the stability of the *Pax Romana*, with immediate evidence of the instability of the times, while it left the world of Greek Christianity relatively unscathed. While perhaps no one in the period, least of all the Latin Christians, foresaw the possibility of a time when Roman power would completely pass from view, the effects of the resettlements were more than sufficient to call into question their claim that a betterment of conditions would flow from the recognition of the Church. Indeed, it was now open to Latin pagans to assert that, on the very grounds on which that claim had been argued, the events of the time proved that the substitution of an impotent Christian God for the deities which had once made

Rome great had been a tragic blunder. To such an argument it was, at least in the first instance, hard to see what Christians could reply.

The first to recognize the critical character of the situation in its full dimensions was the formidable figure of Aurelius Augustinus, Bishop of Hippo Regius in Latin Africa in the early decades of the fifth century. The fact that Augustine's magisterial twenty-two books *On the City of God,* his most comprehensive statement of his mature theological views, should have been undertaken as a reply to pagan interpretations of the sack of Rome by the troops of Alaric in A.D. 410 has perplexed many of its readers. It has been pointed out that the sack itself was far less destructive to the city than those which were to follow, as well as that Augustine's work embodies his views on such pressing matters as the Donatist and Pelagian controversies within its scope. But our discussion of Eusebius and the imperial theologians of the West should leave little doubt as to the crushing blow which even this initial molestation of the ancient imperial capital administered to the Christians of the time; and Augustine's treatise, which admittedly became something of a commonplace book during its long composition between 413 and 426, is to the end an attempt to discern the purposes of God in relation to the crisis which the sack of Rome foreshadowed. In the first part of the work (Books I-X), Augustine undertakes to attack the notion that peace and prosperity are to be expected from the worship of the true God. In the second (XI-XXII), he develops a truly radical view of God's efforts to restore men to the community or "city" of God, which takes its clue from the very circumstances of the time which might seem to cast doubt on Christian claims regarding God's power and rule in the world.

Augustine's great work is best understood, as Professor F. E. Cranz has shown, when it is studied against the background of certain earlier works in which Augustine employs its central themes in different contexts. We may look briefly at two such works here: that *On the True Religion,* in which the notion of two societies confronting one another in the present age first makes its appearance, and that *On Catechizing the Uninstructed,* in which the scriptural theme of the "city of God" is first extensively employed in elaborating this notion.

THE TREATISE ON THE TRUE RELIGION

The little treatise *On the True Religion* dates from A.D. 390, three years after Augustine's baptism at Milan. It was written in Africa, dedicated to an old friend and former patron, as a defense of Christianity as the only *religio*—set of attitudes and practices—which is in conformity with the truth about man's relationship with God. It reflects little of the results of either the intensive scriptural study or the growing acquaintance with the issues of contemporary Greek Christian thought which mark the later writings. But at the same time it is far in advance of the earlier philosophical writings of the former professor of rhetoric who had found little to satisfy him in the Tertullianist Christianity to which he had been slightly exposed in his youth and had only recently been attracted by the views of the converted Neo-Platonist, Gaius Marius Victorinus, and the allegorical preaching of Ambrose at Milan. In fact, the work is the first comprehensive statement of the central themes of the Augustinian theology.

The Platonism through which Augustine had finally been brought to Christianity appears in this work in a form in which most of the subtle reflections on the distortion of the self by false love and self-will which we associate with the mature Augustine are lacking. The human problem is almost crudely stated as the beclouding of the mind by the passions when, in an imaginary conversation, a disciple of Plato is made to ask his master if human weakness is not due to the fact that men are unaware that "the mind has to be healed [of passions] so that it may behold the immutable form of things . . . preserving its beauty unchanged and unchangeable" and whether a person who convinced such men "that the rational and intellectual soul is given to enjoy the contemplation of [God's] eternity" would not be worthy of "divine honors" (*True Religion* III.3). To this proposition Plato replies that such a thing "could not be done by man unless the very virtue and wisdom of God delivered him from his natural environment and illuminated him not by human teaching but internal illumination" (*ibid.*). But, Augustine adds, this is precisely what is "celebrated in books and documents" which record that "from one particular region of the earth in which alone the one God is worshiped and where such a man could be born, chosen men were sent throughout the entire world, and by their virtues and words have kindled the fires of divine love" (III.4). While the theme of love toward God appears in these final words, the formal structure of Augustine's treatment of the human problem which God has met in Christ is a rather dry version of the livelier constructions of the pagan and Christian Greek Platonists.

Even in these passages, however, the peculiar immediacy with which Latin writers invested human events is apparent in Augustine's simple declaration that the perfection of the mind, which is the fundamental need of man, is observably taking place as a result of the work of Christ. Thus he says that, in what he calls the "Christian epoch" (*tempora Christiani*) (III.3), the truths about God "are read to the people throughout all the world and listened to most gladly" (III.5), with the result that many have actually been led to embrace martyrdom and chastity rather than revert to the old way of life. Indeed, he asserts, had Plato lived in this era he would have become a Christian "as many Platonists of recent times have done" (IV.7). It is the arresting evidence of the events of the present which seems to Augustine the compelling ground on which to recommend Christianity.

Augustine further expands his picture of the sweep of events which the world is now witnessing in his discussion of the truth of the Scriptures, which he describes as "the account (*historia*) and prophecy of the temporal dispensation of divine providence for the salvation of the human race through renewal and reform" (VII.13). That is, the purpose of the Scriptures is to describe the steps by which God, who "adopts all kinds of means suitable to the times which are ordered by his marvelous wisdom" (XV.30), finally brought man to the point where "the old servitude had passed and the day of liberty had dawned and man was fitly and helpfully taught how he had been created with free will" with which to emancipate himself under divine guidance (XVI.31). This guidance is now being supplied by Christ, whose "whole life on earth as man . . . was an education in morals . . . adapted to complete the education and exercise of the soul" (XVI.32-XVII.33). The argument, as Augustine develops it, again shows the general effect of Greek philosophical and theological ideas in its sketch of God's action as the education of the soul. But again the argument is informed with that fascination with the unfolding course of events as such which is characteristic of so many Latin works.

The reason for lingering over these early manifestations of the Latin mood in Augustine's work is the light which they shed on the notion of two societies juxtaposed in the present age, the most original of his arguments, which now follows. The achievement of perfection for the soul, he insists, is part of a universal design, since "divine providence not only looks after individuals, as it were privately, but also after the whole race publicly" (XXV.46). Indeed, the dispensation of God described in the Scriptures can be thought of on an analogy between the life of the race as a whole and the classic seven stages of man's life from infancy, through manhood, to death (XXVII.48). But at this point Augustine moves very quickly from a reference to the "old or exterior or earthly man," to which this analogy applies, to a more extensive discussion of the seven stages in the perfection of "the new man, the inward and heavenly man," as he is being brought from the stage of reliance on "the histories which nourish by examples" to the actual attainment of "total forgetfulness of temporal life, passing into the perfect form which is made according to the image and likeness of God," and then finally to the "eternal rest and perpetual beatitude with no distinguishable ages" (XXVII.49). Thus, he summarizes, there are "two classes" confronting one another:

> In one of these is the multitude of the impious who bear the image of the earthly man from the beginning to the end of the age. In the other is the succession of the people devoted to the one God. . . . (But) if any of the earthly people . . . had the merit of reaching the illumination of the inward man, [God] gave to the human race in his day his aid, showing it what the age required, hinting by prophecy what it was not opportune to show clearly (XXVII.50-51).

Augustine is not at his clearest in applying the idea of the seven stages in the life of a man to the "old or exterior or earthly man," and he could even be thought to hold a Millenarian idea, of the sort he later rejected, that a seventh earthly age would intervene before the end of the world. But the point is that the analogy itself serves Augustine as a means of fusing his interest in the perfection of the soul, which he here describes in simple Platonic terms as the achievement of perfect form, with his own perception of this goal as the end of an actual course of events unfolding before men. In this fusion was born in this early work the notion of two societies juxtaposed in this age, which was to remain central to his thought in its later form as well.

It is instructive to compare the treatise *On the True Religion* with Tertullian's *Apology*, to which it bears a striking resemblance in general form as well as an equally striking lack of resemblance in contents. Augustine's route to Christianity was one which led away from Tertullian's insistence on simple obedience to the divine will toward a more subtle view of the perfection of man. But the same route also led away from the kind of immediate concern with the operation of divine providence which was Tertullian's legacy to such Latin imperial theologians as Lactantius. The analogy between the life of the human race and that of man is a case in point here, since it places emphasis on the general issues of human life rather than on particular happenings. But Augustine's references to *historia* are another case in point. In the passages already cited, the term denotes something more than a certain department of intellectual endeavor. It is a record of the living course of events which fascinated Augustine no less than other pagan and Christian Latins. But in the treatment of the stages of the life of the "new, inward, and heavenly man" the scriptural histories serve chiefly to furnish human examples to be followed in the early stages of spiritual development.

Later in the work, Augustine takes up the subject again in a discussion which is chiefly concerned with reviewing the standard arguments of the allegorists against those who place too much stress on such absurdities as the literal references of the Scriptures to God's hands and feet (L.99). Augustine's remarks are of special interest, since his main purpose is not to defend allegorical interpretation but to assert that such aspects of ancient accounts must not obscure their importance as food for the mind (LI.100). Indeed, he here foreshadows the justly famous treatment of the past available to the memory as the means of interpreting the living relationship of man and God, which Augustine was to launch in the tenth book of *Confessions*. In its present context, however, the discussion is such as to divert attention once again from the specific issue of the providential meaning of events which were as much the province of the historian as the theologian—the issue which we have seen raised in principle in Tertullian and his fourth-century heirs. Thus, while this treatise foreshadows Augustine's later handling of the problems created by the disasters of his age, it also shows how far removed he was at this time from any such concern with the concrete meaning of the events in which the fortunes of the Church and the empire were enmeshed such as that shown by his Latin Christian predecessors and contemporaries.

THE TREATISE ON CATECHIZING THE UNINSTRUCTED

The ten years between the treatise *On the True Religion* (A.D. 390) and *On Catechizing the Uninstructed* (A.D. 400) were perhaps the most creative in Augustine's theological development. It was in this period that he first advanced (e.g., *Letter to Simplician* I-II) his classic interpretation of Paul's Letter to the Romans as having fundamentally to do with the psychological fact that a divinely imposed obligation (law) is ineffectual in accomplishing the salvation of a man whose self-orientation is not reversed by the renovating power of God (grace). Such an argument was already conventional with Greek Christians, but its development in the light of the overarching Latin concern with salvation as dependent on man's response to the issues confronting him marked the virtual creation of the "Paul" who has survived into medieval and modern times. Moreover, the same period brought forth Augustine's *Confessions*, the remarkable work in which he used his "Paul" in retelling how God had acted in the events of his own past to destroy his self-orientation and to recreate him as an obedient doer of God's will. Not least of the reasons for the intensive scriptural studies of the period, as well as for the further exploration of contemporary Greek Christian thought which we are now increasingly aware accompanied them, was the fact that Augustine was now propelled into the unwonted position of bishop of the principal port city of Numidia, Hippo Regius, and was thus numbered among those responsible for the defense and exposition of the Christian faith.

It was in this new capacity that he found himself in the position of advising a deacon of the Carthaginian Church in the techniques to be employed in giving a group of catechumens their first instruction in the faith. The result was the attractive little treatise *On Catechizing the Uninstructed,* in the course of which the notion of the two societies of men is elaborated in terms of the scriptural theme of Jerusalem or "the city of God."

The effects of the intervening decade on Augustine's thought are everywhere apparent in the treatise. The central object of the catechist, whose task it is to recount for his hearers the work of God from the beginning to the "present epoch of the Church (*tempora ecclesiae*)" (III.5), is, he insists, to awake in them an awareness of the love which God has concretely shown to men and so to arouse an answering love which will mitigate their pride. It must be made clear, he says, that

the same Lord Jesus Christ, God-Man, is at once a token of divine love towards us and an example among us of man's lowliness, to the end that great as is our swelling of evil (*magnus tumor*), it may be healed by an even greater medicine. For it is a great misery—a proud man. But it is a greater mercy—a humble God. . . . With this love, therefore, set before you as the end to which you refer all that you say, so give all your instruction that he to whom you speak by hearing may believe, and by believing hope, and by hoping love (IV.8).

The similarity between this statement of purpose and that which underlies Augustine's "confessions" of the events through which God entered his own life (*Confessions* X.4) is even clearer in the statement that the catechist must see his words as "stamping certain impressions . . . upon the memory" (II.3). The deacon's *narratio* or recitation of God's actions is virtually itself an event through which God's grace works salvation.

Augustine's further remarks on methodology, as they flow from this initial view of the deacon's task, take the form of sage and even humorous observations on the circumstances in which this purpose must be fulfilled. It is not necessary, he points out, to repeat to the catechumens "the whole Pentateuch, the whole book of Judges, and Kings, and Esdras, and the whole Gospel and Acts of the Apostles" but only the more memorable and arresting evidence of God's work which they provide (*Catechizing* III.5). After all, he pursues, the Scriptures written before Christ had for their purpose "to announce his coming and to prefigure the Church to be, that is to say, the people of God throughout all nations, which Church is his body, in which are included and numbered all the just who ever lived in this world even before his coming and who believed that he would come as we believe that he has come" (III.6). The theme of Augustine's words—and it is the same as that which underlies his subtle suggestions as to how the insights of rhetoric may be used in discerning the diverse purposes and spiritual aptitudes of those who come to hear the *narratio* (VIII-XV)—is that the catechist must fascinate his hearers with the actions of God in their behalf, as those actions have unfolded from the past into the present. And it is to this same theme that he reverts at the end of the specimen address which fills the latter part of the work, when he says:

> All these things, then, we know have come to pass exactly as they were foretold long ago. . . . So we, because all these things have been fulfilled . . . are edified unto faith, that waiting and persevering in the Lord, we believe without hesitation that the things, likewise, which yet remain shall come to pass, since we read in the same scriptures of tribulations yet to come, and of the last day of judgment itself . . . (XXIV.45).

The statement is, of course, a virtual reproduction of Tertullian's argument that the fulfillment of the rest of the scriptural prophecies is sure because of the evidence of those already fulfilled (cf. *Apology* XX). Its novel aspect is its special emphasis on the faith which the entire unfolding of God's work should arouse. It is an emphasis explained in part by the particular purpose with which Augustine writes, but in part also by his special interest in the nature of the human response to God.

Allusions to the theme of the "city of God" appear throughout the treatise. In discussing the final stages of the *narratio*, Augustine mentions that reference is to be made "with eager longing (to) the kingdom of the righteous and faithful, and to that city and its joys" (VII.11). Moreover, the passage just quoted from his own specimen address refers to the day of judgment as that when "all the citizens of both (the) cities shall receive again their bodies and rise and shall render an account of their life before the judgment-seat of Christ" (XXIV.45). But it is in the midst of the address, and in connection with the apologetic problem of the continuation of evil in the midst of the creation, that Augustine chiefly unveils the new form in which he has cast his notion of the juxtaposition of two societies in the present age. Thus he explains that evil continues not because God is powerless to prevent it but because

> there are two cities, one of the wicked, the other of the just, which are being carried down from the beginning of the human race to the end of

the age, and which arc now intermingled in body but separated in will, and which are, moreover, to be separated in body also on the day of judgment (XIX.31).

The one, he continues, is composed of men "who love pride and temporal rule . . . and all spirits who set their affections on such things and seek their own glory in the subjection of men," the other of men and spirits "who humbly seek God's glory and not their own, and who follow him in godliness" (*ibid.*).

Augustine is now more specific as to the events through which the intermingled life of the two cities can be traced. Referring more or less obviously to Hebrews 11:8-10 and Galatians 4:21-31, he says that it was with Abraham that there first appeared a people in whom "the coming Church was prefigured," since they "thought of the future rest, and looked longingly for the heavenly fatherland" which God was ultimately to reveal with the coming of Christ. Among the signs and symbols with which that people were invested was Jerusalem, "that celebrated city of God, which, while in bondage, served as a sign (*signo*) of that free city which is called heavenly Jerusalem, a Hebrew word which means 'vision of peace' " (XX.36). Moreover, he adds (cf. Rev. 14:8; 17:1-18:24), a second city was introduced later with the captivity of this same people in Babylon, so that "as Jerusalem signifies the city and fellowship of the righteous, so Babylon signifies the city and fellowship of the unrighteous, since it is said to signify 'confusion' " (XXI.37). The meaning of these cities is that "the Church of Christ present in all his saints, who are citizens of the heavenly Jerusalem, was to be in bondage under the rulers of this age," though it is now a fact that, in consequence of the prayers of Christians on their behalf, "through these very rulers peace was given to the Church, albeit temporal peace, temporal quietude for the spiritual building of houses and planting of gardens and vineyards" (*ibid.*).

Two things have happened to the notion of the two societies juxtaposed in the present age since the writing of the treatise *On the True Religion*. In the first place, Augustine has seen fit to elaborate his views through the use of the scriptural theme of the "city of God." It is not surprising that he should do so in view of the increasingly scriptural orientation of his thought. This is not, of course, a new theme for early Christian writers. Quite apart from the use of references to Jerusalem found in the New Testament, continued attention is paid to it by Greek Christians as a means of describing the coming life with God—we have noted the deviation from this theme found in Eusebius' application of the scriptural references to the "city of God" to the divine *politeia* inaugurated by Constantine. Nor is Augustine's amplification of this theme by the introduction of a second city, Babylon, entirely new, since his association of references to it in Revelation with those from Hebrews and Galatians had already been found in the works of Tyconius, a former Donatist theologian who had secluded himself on his African estates after his break with his onetime associates.

But a second development in Augustine's notion of the two societies, equally apparent here, is its accommodation to his new understanding of the human problem as that of self-orientation— of pride and of self-will—and of its resolution through God's incorporation of men in the humble and self-effacing life of Christ. The references here made to the rest and peace of the heavenly city, as well as to the pride and strife of the earthly city, so obviously incorporate the familiar terms in which this understanding is articulated in *Confessions* (e.g., I.1; II.6; III.8; VI.16) as to need no comment.

Several things need to be said, however, about the light which this work—as read against the background of that *On the True Religion*—sheds on the later development of Augustine's views. Thus it may be observed as one peculiar result of Augustine's Latin adaptations of Greek Christian ideas that he thinks of the new life of communion with Christ as so clearly combining present fulfillment and future promise that its fundamentally eschatological character is often obscured. In the present treatise, for example, he distinguishes between those who lived "before his coming" from those who "believe that he has come" (*Catechizing* III.6) with such ease that he might seem to have excluded all notions of a future coming of Christ from his considerations. This has, indeed, been the assumption of many who have read his views in the form in which they appear later in the treatise *On the City of God*. But quite apart from Augustine's use of Tertullian's argument regarding the certainty of the fulfillment of future prophecies and his reference to the judgment of Christ yet to come, it should be clear from this work that every reference to the coming of Christ is a reference to the immediate presence of a life which is to be lived in its fullness only in the future. Augustine's peculiar foreshortening of the distance between present and future is, in fact, a result of the transformation of the contemporary Greek Christian interest in the achievement of perfection by the soul into a characteristically Latin Christian call to heed the challenge posed by present events.

The other thing which needs to be said, however, is that, while Augustine's concentration on the Scriptures here combines with his reflection on God's action in his own life to give him a much more concrete frame of reference in which to view the course of the two societies juxtaposed in the present, he is as yet unconcerned with the broader course of events with which the Latin imperial theologians had involved themselves. Augustine does actually refer, almost as an afterthought, to the fact that the rulers of the earthly city have been led by the prayers of the Christians to grant a temporal kind of peace to the Church (XXI.37). Placed in the context of the ideas of the time, this reference is perhaps more in the nature of an acceptance of the views of his contemporaries than anything else. But, in fact, at this juncture in his career the Bishop of Hippo Regius, civic official though he was, had little—and little good— to say about the *imperium*, which he saw as an embodiment of the scriptural figure of Babylon. This is a striking, negative witness to the gulf which separates both this work and its predecessor from its successor, in which Augustine perforce had to say very much indeed about the subject.

THE TWENTY-TWO BOOKS
ON THE CITY OF GOD

We may return now to Augustine's great work with, hopefully, several things accomplished. The treatise *On the City of God* is not the first work in which the exegetical theme of Jerusalem was explored, nor the first in which Augustine himself had employed the theme in the elaboration of his notion of two societies juxtaposed in the present age. What distinguishes the work from its predecessors, when the frequent asides and extensive digressions which result in part from the circumstances of its composition are taken into account, is its application of Augustine's view to the crisis of the Christian empire of which he was made concretely aware by the pagan criticism that arose in the wake of the sack of Rome. The occasion, which has often seemed little more than a pretext, actually explains the unique place of the work among his writings.

It is only in the second part of the work that Augustine seriously undertakes the task, which he defines as that of dealing with the scriptural theme of the "origin, . . . relationship, . . . and destinies" of the two cities currently mixed with each other in the present age (*duarum civitatum quas in hoc interim saeculo perplexas exortu et excursu et debitis finibus*) (XI.1). His statement of purpose illustrates that view of theology as scriptural exegesis which he held as an increasingly apt student of his Greek Christian contemporaries, though here again his own practice is closer to the earlier typological or testimonial tradition inherited by Tertullian and common to the Latin West. In any case, his rigid conformity to the program which he sets himself provides an obvious scheme for discussing how his full-developed view of the origin (XI-XIV), the relationship (XV-XVIII), and the destinies (XIX-XXII) of the two cities differs from that found in his earlier writings.

THE ORIGINS OF THE CITIES

The characteristics which make the work a virtual synthesis of Augustine's theological ideas appear at once in his discussion of the origins of the two cities. Allowing himself the widest latitude, Augustine opens his discussion with an interpretation of the creation narrative in Genesis, chapter 1, in which he is at pains to distinguish the eternity and infinity of the triune God from the temporality and finitude of the spiritual and physical creatures (XI.4-XII.5). The argument, pursued at almost wearisome length, follows much the same line as that found in Augustine's treatise *On the Trinity*, written between A.D. 399 and 419, and shows many of the same similarities to the cosmological views with which the Cappadocian fathers had defended the Neo-Nicene formulas regarding the triune God. In fact, Augustine here shows that recurrent tendency of Latin writers, pagan and Christian, to adopt the intellectual formulations of their Greek contemporaries almost as a matter of course.

The equally recurrent tendency of Latin writers to adapt such formulations to their own purposes shortly appears, however, when Augustine turns to the fall of the angels, the commonly accepted prelude to any discussion of the fall of Adam through the machinations of Satan. The fall of the angels was no irrelevant matter for Augustine's Greek Christian contemporaries, since it confronted them directly with the problem of explaining the defection of a purely spiritual nature without reference to the physical order. For Augustine, however, this perplexing problem is simply the occasion for the assertion that there is no reason why such spiritual creatures, blessed as they are above both animals and men, should have rebelled against their creator (XII.6-7). Their defection is the result of their error in confusing the creation with the creator. Thus they conceived a misguided love for themselves rather than God, and so fell heir to the malice, pride, and confusion which flows from the following a lesser good: "Consequently he who inordinately loves the good which any nature possesses . . . himself becomes evil in the good and wretched because deprived of a greater good" (XII.18). What Augustine has done is to employ the distinction between the eternal and infinite God and his temporal and finite creatures as a means of rewriting the drama of creation and fall in the light of the understanding of sin to which he had come through his earlier reflections on the human problem. The unique feature of his argument does not lie so much in any specific difference between his cosmology and that of his Greek Christian contemporaries as in the quite different context in which he appropriates their views.

It is this same tendency which appears as Augustine turns to discuss the unfolding periods of time which will extend to the end of the creation and in which God's purposes are to be fulfilled. His discussion is prefaced by his famous attack on any notion of a limitless time or of the recurrence of happenings within it (XII.10-15), and it is in this connection that he attacks the notion of a "cycle of times" (*circuitus temporum*) for which he stigmatizes the philosophers (XII.14). This is the attack, of course, which has so frequently been cited in justification of a Greek "cyclic view of history." Its importance is very different. Augustine's conception of the creation as bounded by periods of time is a rough approximation of the notion of the succession of time-intervals (Gk.: *diastemata*) accompanying the movements of the ordered cosmos which served the Cappadocian fathers as a means of distinguishing the eternal Godhead from the temporal creation. At Augustine's hands this notion has become the background against which a picture of the inexorable movement of God's purposes, which are at work despite the defection of the angelic beings, can be presented in all its grandeur. The attack on the *circuitus temporum* as obscuring that movement is of interest, not because it has anything to do with Augustine's understanding of *historia* but because it sheds light on the function which his inherited conception of time actually plays in his thought.

It is as an extension of these observations on the fall of the angels and the certain fulfillment of God's purposes which even that event cannot forestall that Augustine at last deals with the fall of Adam and the punishment of death which was God's answer to it (XIII.1-XIV.27). It was by an appeal to the pride of self that Satan tempted Adam to turn from God and brought upon him the domination of the passions which results in the loss of the power to control his lower appetites. Augustine here cites his version of the text "Pride is the beginning of sin" (Ecclesiasticus 10:13) and inquires:

> What is pride but the craving of undue exaltation? And this is undue exaltation, when the soul abandons him whom it should cleave to as its own end and becomes a kind of end in itself. This happens when it becomes its own satisfaction. And it does so when it falls away from that unchangeable good which ought to satisfy it more than itself. This falling away is spontaneous; for if the will had remained stedfast in the love of that higher and changeless good . . . it would not have turned away to find satisfaction in itself (XIV.13).

This description of sin is, in one sense, no more than a restatement of Augustine's earlier views. Its novelty lies in the fact that it is now set in the wider context provided by the discussion of the angelic fall and the inevitable triumph of God's plans. A full consideration of Augustine's views would show that here again he is dependent on notions derived in particular from the Cappadocian fathers, particularly in his treatment of the good intent and temporary nature of the decree of death (XIV.15; cf. XIII.1-19) and of the necessary function performed in bringing the creation to perfection through procreation despite the lust which entered the sexual act as a result of the fall (XIV.10-26). But these matters are ultimately irrelevant to Augustine's purpose. What Augustine has done is to establish what he thinks to be the necessary background against which the further description of God's purposes in his dealings with men must be set. With the triumph of Satan over Adam and the passing of the decree of death, the community of those who love God and whose will is obedient to him is reduced to that of the unfallen angels, yet the inevitable triumph of God's purposes is not in doubt. It is in this context that we must understand the classic passage in which he finally introduces the theme of the two cities by saying that the outcome of the struggle of Satan and God was the distinguishing of a community based on love of self (that of fallen angels and sons of Adam) from a community based on love of God (that of the unfallen angels):

> Accordingly two cities have been formed by two loves: the earthly by love of self even to the contempt of God, the heavenly by the love of God even to the contempt of self. . . . In the one, the princes and the nations it subdues are ruled by the love of ruling; in the other, the princes and the subjects serve one another in love. . . . And therefore the wise men of the one city, living according to man, have sought for profit to their own bodies or souls . . . and those who have known God "glorified him not as God, neither were thankful but became vain in their own imaginations, and their foolish heart was darkened, professing themselves to be wise" (Romans 1:21-25). But in the other city there is no human wisdom, but only godliness, which offers due worship toward God and looks for its reward to the society of the saints (XIV.28).

Should there be any question that the purpose of this section of the work is ultimately dictated by the crisis of the Christian empire, it should be dispelled by these references to the leaders of the nations, as well as by the restriction, almost cruel in the circumstances, of the "due worship of God" to the citizens of the city of God. What Augustine has tried to do in Books XI-XIV is treat the origin of the two societies which he has long regarded as juxtaposed in the present age in such a way that no room is left for the notion that the worship of the true God by the city of this world is likely to effect any change in its fortunes. That city is a product of the rebellion against God which has already been punished by the decree of death against the sons of Adam. It is more than doubtful whether the final triumph of the purposes of God will involve in any way the betterment of its condition.

THE RELATIONS OF THE CITIES

The section of Augustine's work which has been hardest to understand where its relation to the crisis of the Christian empire has not been taken into account is that which he carefully redefines as concerned with "the course of these two cities . . . through the whole time or age in which the dying give place and those who are born succeed" (XV.1). In fact, it is precisely in this section that he most pointedly develops his earlier notion of two societies juxtaposed in the present age in such a way as to give a different meaning to the disasters of his time from that on which the claims of the imperial theologians were based.

The development which Augustine's views have undergone since he wrote the treatise *On Catechizing the Uninstructed* emerges at once in the interpretation of the Pauline distinction (Gal. 4:21-31) between the sons of Abraham by Hagar and Sarah —children of flesh and promise, citizens of the present Jerusalem and that to come—with which this section opens (*City* XV.1-3). In his earlier work, he had loosely identified Abraham's spiritual sons with Israel as a whole (*Catechizing* XX.36). However, he now attempts a more subtle distinction. Lest no witness to the heavenly city should be left in all the reaches of the world governed by sin and death, he argues, God chose one of the nations of men to be not only the earthly city which it was by its own nature but also an image of the heavenly city which he willed to re-establish among his creatures. Thus the city of Jerusalem filled a dual function, that of "its own obvious presence and its symbolic representation of the heavenly city" (*City* XV.2). Much of Israel's life, therefore, is simply the life of the earthly city, "which shall not be everlasting . . . , has its good in this age, and rejoices in it with such joy as it can afford" (*ibid.*). But throughout its existence, Israel also served, in a fashion unrecognized by most, as the custodian of a city which foreshadowed the heavenly Jerusalem to come. With Abraham in particular (XVI.26-32) there began to appear a spiritual succession of those who, recognizing the real intentions of God, looked forward in faith to a fulfillment of the coming of that city of which Jerusalem could only be an image. Those who stood in this succession saw "many things concerning Christ and the kingdom of heaven, which is the city of God" (XVII.2); but it is by anticipation only that they have a place among the citizens of the heavenly city, which has now actually begun to manifest itself among those who acknowledge Christ.

It is not surprising that Augustine's purpose in this section should have remained obscure to many of his readers, since the course of his argument is complicated by an almost bewildering series of observations on the course of the city of this world. These include such proofs of the imperfection of the earthly city of which Israel is a representative as his reference to Rome as founded by a fratricide (XV.5), a more extensive treatment of Israel's own part in the affairs of the ancient Near Eastern empires (XV.5-27), and a discussion, certainly more elaborate than revealing, of the cause of Alexander's ascendancy over both the Greeks and the orientals (XVIII.2-27). When set against his earlier writings and the circumstances of the time, however, his intentions leap forth at points too numerous to mention, as when he surveys the disputes of the Jews over the antiquity and adequacy of their Scriptures (cf. Tertullian, *Apology* XXI) as evidence that "it was not possible that the nations would expect [Christ] to come, as they did, to do justice in the splendor of power, unless they should first believe in him when he came to suffer judgment in the humility of patience" (*City* XVIII.45). Nor are his intentions obscure when he attacks the Arian emperors of the later Constantinian and Valentinian periods equally with the Arian Goths for their persecution of the Catholics (XVIII.52-54). What he is concerned to point out at every turn, to establish by every means at his disposal, is that Israel itself—and therefore every other nation—belongs to the realm of sin and death which he has earlier seen as having its origins at the very beginning of things. As part of what is still "Babylon" (XVIII.52), it is the inevitable victim rather than the beneficiary of the emergence of the heavenly city in Christ and his followers.

Augustine's purpose is perfectly clear. While it is hard to establish any concrete knowledge of the interpretation which Eusebius himself had given to the scriptural theme of Jerusalem,

Augustine's treatment of this theme is so pointedly opposite to it as to leave no doubt that he is developing his earlier views with those of the imperial theologians and their critics in mind. In effect, his message is that no reader of the Scriptures should ever have imagined that there could again be room in God's purposes for a restoration of the earthly Jerusalem. That city once served as an image and foreshadowing of the heavenly city. But with the coming of Christ there is no need for such an image, since the reality of which it was the image is now beginning to appear in the world. What this of course means concretely, in terms of the events of the time, is that those who think that the Roman empire should expect that peace and security to result from its worship of the true God are tragically in error. If Israel itself belonged to the realm of sin and death, the empire has little to hope for, since the special function which Israel once performed is no longer needed. As he says in conclusion to this section, "both (cities) alike either enjoy temporal good things or are afflicted with temporal evils, but with diverse faith, diverse hope, and diverse love, until they must be separated by the last judgment and each receive her own end, of which there is no end" (XVIII.54).

There is, therefore, much more than first meets the eye in the new distinction between the two functions of Israel in God's purposes as it makes its appearance in this work. Indeed, when his chaotic presentation of evidence is taken into account it becomes even more obvious than before that Augustine is seeking a solution to the crisis of the Christian empire which avoids the inexorable logic of both his Christian associates and their pagan critics.

THE ENDS OF THE CITIES

Much of Augustine's discussion of the destinies of the two cities is given over to treating Christian views of the resurrection of the body and the last judgment (XX), the physical punishment of the damned (XXI), and the perpetual rest of the blessed (XXII), particular attention being paid in each case to the objections which these views were bound to encounter from pagans. Here Augustine once again shows himself familiar not only with previous Latin Christian ideas but with the issues currently debated among his Greek Christian contemporaries. His treatment of these matters is perhaps less closely related to the main purpose of the work than are the cosmological views discussed earlier.

At the outset, however, Augustine offers his most important statement of the distinction between the two cities and his final word on their present relationship as he has come to understand it (XIX). The point of departure for his remarks are the philosophical views of the highest good as summarized in the lost treatise *On Philosophy* of the celebrated Latin intellectual of the late Republic, Marcus Terentius Varro (XIX.1-3). For Varro, himself, the basis for judging between the several main views which he distilled from the varieties of philosophical opinion had been man's dual nature as composed of both soul and body, his own conclusion being that virtue in the soul combined with such bodily excellence as nature provides is the sum of human happiness (XIX.3). For Augustine, using Varro's work as a foil for his own argument, the entire philosophical discussion is marred by the fact that it seeks a reduced form of the supreme good not available in the present age and is then tragically confronted with the elusive character of even the good which it seeks (XIX.4). It is the Christian, of whom it is said that "the just live by faith," who has been given a vision of the perfect harmony or peace of soul and body, of man personally and socially, who can see what the philosophers dimly perceive because he perceives it not as a possibility in the earthly city that now is but as a certainty in the heavenly city which will be (XIX.4-5, 10-11, 13). But the life which flows from this vision requires the Christian to abandon where necessary even those evidences of a proximate good to which the philosophers cling in order to achieve the supreme good which he anticipates:

> Since, then, the supreme good of the city of God is perfect and eternal peace, not such as mortals pass into and out of by birth and death, but the

peace of freedom from all evil, in which the immortals [i.e., the angels] ever abide, who can deny that that future life is most blessed, or that, in comparison with it, this life which we now live is most wretched, be it filled with all the blessings of soul and body and external things? And yet, if any man uses this life with a reference to that other which he ardently loves and confidently hopes for, he may well be called even now blessed, though not in reality so much as in hope (XIX.20).

Even without reference to what we shall soon see was Augustine's use of Varro as a commentator on Roman paganism in the first part of the work, his purpose in using Varro's work at this point is not at all hard to discern. That purpose is not merely to establish an abstract contrast between the fruitless search for an earthly good and the reality of the supreme good. It is to set over against an impossible dream of a *Pax Romana* the concrete hope of the coming peace of the city of God. The bulk of his illustrations of the fruitlessness of the search for an earthly good are drawn from the Roman past. He notes that Cicero, in his *On Consolation,* could only lament over the death of his daughter, disrupting his soul with grief because he knew of no life without physical decay; and he adds that the suicide of Cato shows that the virtue of fortitude is no less prey to the corruptions of this life (XIX.4). Again, he is at pains to show that, while the philosophers are right in seeing the good life as social rather than merely personal, not even the empire, itself victim of many internal discords, can claim to unite the whole world in the good life which they describe (XIX.6-13). Indeed, he subsequently argues that the Roman *respublica* for which Scipio spoke in Cicero's *On the Commonwealth* cannot be shown to have existed except as an ideal (XIX.21). The form of Augustine's discussion once again shows that his ideas have taken the particular character they now assume out of a concern to transcend the logic which has confounded his Christian associates in the face of pagan recriminations over the present course of events.

It is in the light of this underlying purpose that we must in-

terpret Augustine's famous description of the relation of the two
cities and the earthly and heavenly peace which seeks:

> The earthly city, which does not live by faith seeks an earthly peace,
> and the end it proposes in the well-ordered concord of civic obedience and
> rule, is the combination of men's wills to attain the things which are helpful
> to this life. The heavenly city, or rather the part of it which sojourns on
> earth and lives by faith, makes use of this peace only because it must, until
> this mortal condition which necessitates it shall pass away. Consequently, so
> long as it lives like a captive and a stranger in the earthly city . . . it makes
> no scruple to obey the laws of the earthly city . . . and thus . . . there is
> a harmony between them in regard to what belongs to it (XIX.17).

When recognized for what it is, this statement is Augustine's final
word on the nature of the Christian empire. It is not a divine
politeia, nor the herald of a new age of peace and security, but a
pragmatic union of two entities essentially different in their ideals
and destined for two quite different ends. For Augustine, the disasters of the present do not render that empire devoid of meaning;
but neither do they cast doubt on the reality of the God whose
purposes have led to its formation.

THE FIRST TEN BOOKS—AND SOME
REMARKS ON HISTORIA

When Augustine began to write of the origin, re-
lation, and ends of the two cities, he had already issued the almost
equally massive ten books in refutation of pagan religion which
form the first part of the completed work. Augustine was later to
describe these books as forming, in effect, a negative background to
the positive statement of his teaching on the two cities (*Retractions*
II.43), and there is every reason to think that the general scheme of
the completed work, including the three sections of the second
part, was already in his mind at the outset (cf. *City* I.*praef.*, 35).
But there is equally good reason to think that Augustine did not
initially contemplate a work of such massive proportions as finally
emerged. At the outset he speaks of an account of the earthly city

as almost incidental to his purposes (I.*praef.*). Even at the end of the first book he sets out the scope of things to come in what is in retrospect an almost humorous reference to "somewhat" (*quaedam*) more which he has to say on the subject (I.36). It is only at the beginning of the second book that the grand scale of what is to follow is suggested by an apologetic statement that criticism of what he has already said will require a lengthier discussion than might otherwise be desirable (II.1).

But there is another aspect to this matter, at once more perplexing and even more important. The argument of the first book is what we might expect from the treatise *On Catechizing the Uninstructed*, where we have seen no tendency either to accept the notion of new possibilities open before what Augustine baldly refers to as "Babylon" or to deny the general principle on which the thought of the imperial theologians rested (*Catechizing* XXI.37). Thus Augustine not only argues that the sack of Rome destroyed merely temporal goods (I.10-14) and purged Rome of evils deplored by pagan and Christian alike (I.24-33), but also insists that the event was less destructive than it would have been had not the Goths been Arian Christians and is itself thus a virtual witness to the power of Christ (I.1-7). The latter suggestion is interesting on more than one count, but at the moment it is sufficient to observe that it is most easily understood as a form of the argument that Rome's condition has been bettered with the coming of Christianity. Moreover, we know that as late as A.D. 416 Augustine suggested that his disciple, Orosius, produce a work to show that the ancient empires had suffered worse disasters than those which had befallen Rome, a project which is again most easily understood as involving acceptance of the imperial theological principle, as Orosius' own *Seven Books of History Against the Pagans* essentially do.

The point here is not to suggest that Augustine ever agreed with the imperial theologians but, rather, that he began his work with little realization of the problems or the possibilities which were inherent in the task he set himself. If so, it will help to explain the peculiarity of Augustine's treatment of Roman *historia* with

which much of the first ten books is concerned and which foreshadows the developed view of the two cities presented in the
second part of the work.

There are two tendencies which run through Augustine's
treatment of this evidence. One is what we may call the political,
and is that inherited from earlier Christian efforts to show that the
Christian God rather than the pagan deities controls Rome's destiny.
The other we may call the psychological, and is uniquely Augustinian in character. Neither strain is fully distinguishable from
the other, but each is identifiable in all that Augustine has to say.
For example, in the second and third books, which form a single
unit and presumably appeared together, Augustine advances the
view that the pagan deities, by not inculcating morals in the
Romans (II.4-13), "took no steps to prevent the people who worshiped them from being overwhelmed by . . . calamities but
rather aggravated their ruin" (III.1). The point he attempts to make
is recognizably the same as Tertullian's view that Rome's rise to
greatness has some other explanation than its devotion to the pagan
deities (III.17-31). But it differs in its argument that Rome at its
best has sought, as did Cicero in his *On the Commonwealth,* to
establish in fact the harmonious *respublica* which Plato had en-
visioned (II.14, 21) and has thus been betrayed by pagan worship
from achieving its goal. In the course of his argument, he refers
constantly to Sallust, to the effect that his foolish talk about the
restoration of antique morality simply served to obscure the fact
that the impulse to virtue which he rightly saw as necessary to the
health of the *respublica* was not available in his time (II.18-20;
III.16-28). The conclusion, drawn on the basis of a review of the
corruption of Rome from historical sources for the most part, is
that it is by accepting the Christ whose moral teachings have affected even the Arian Goths that Rome's desire for needed virtue
can be fulfilled (II.28-29; III.30-31). The conclusion might well
be a new version of that of the imperialists, except that Augustine
nowhere holds out hope for a new age of peace or prosperity but
only issues a call to find in the Christian life the true fulfillment of
what has hitherto been falsely sought elsewhere.

A similar line of thought is pursued in the fourth and fifth books, with which the discussion of Rome is substantially brought to an end and in which Augustine defends the familiar thesis of his predecessors that it is the true God and not the pagan deities whose purposes are being served in Rome's world dominion. After an examination of the complexity and confusion of the cults reminiscent of Tertullian (IV.7-27), Augustine goes so far here as to assert that "if these gods . . . were unknown . . . and [the true God] alone was known and worshiped with sincere faith and virtue, [the Romans] would have a better kingdom here . . . and might receive an eternal kingdom hereafter" (IV.28). Moreover, after citing both Cicero and Varro against superstition and claiming their philosophical monotheism as a witness (IV.30-31), he asserts the equally familiar Tertullianist point that the pagan gods are demons seeking Rome's ruin (IV.32), but then asserts that while the true God controls all destinies he offers blessedness only to his elect (IV.33), and that much of the scriptural record is given over to proving that he controls "these earthly good things, after which those pant who cannot imagine better things" (IV.33). Against this background we must also set the account which is subsequently given of the self-sacrifice, search for glory, and patriotism of the Romans (V.12-20). While these virtues should challenge Christians, even the philosophers have seen that the Romans themselves were misguided in their search for earthly blessings alone (V.20). Indeed, these virtues are the more arresting insofar as they are not grounded on the recognition that the true God controls human affairs without respect to them, granting mere temporal success even to Christian emperors such as Constantine and Theodosius merely to show who actually controls human life (V.21-26). Here even more clearly than before Augustine shows himself to be reinterpreting inherited themes, which might be taken to be imperialist in character, to his own purposes—the blessings conferred on Christian Rome are real, but they are no more than a witness to blessings of a quite different order of reality.

The residue of Augustine's discussion in these books is concerned with those who think that the worship of the pagan deities will bring deferred spiritual rather than immediate physical rewards (VI-X), and is of singular importance because it clearly juxtaposes for the first time his own notion of the life to come with that based on the assumption held in common by his Christian and pagan contemporaries. Moreover, his discussion is of interest because of its use of the distinction propounded in Varro's *Antiquities Human and Divine* between mythical, civic, and philosophical religion as the point of departure for passing to the more subtle forms of pagan thought which now engage his attention (VI.2-9). By this point, however, the peculiarities of his position are already clear. That position does not so much deny the main contentions of the imperialists as it does convert them to a purpose for which they were not intended. God is responsible for Rome's greatness, he concludes, because he seeks to witness through it to a greater dominion which is not in Rome's grasp. But even this is not so much a carefully reasoned view as it is a merger of two tendencies in Augustine's mind, the one toward accepting the providential nature of events as his predecessors had done and the other toward the peculiar kind of analysis of the self which is the hallmark of his own thought. For this reason it is important to recognize these books as occupying a kind of middle ground between his initial notion that the objections of the pagans could be easily dismissed and his later elaboration of the complex relation between the two societies now juxtaposed in the present age.

Augustine's treatment of Rome is crucial for understanding his whole position. Comments on his work have run the full gamut from the claim that he was unconcerned with concrete events to the notion that he was the author of the first Christian philosophy of history. In fact, there can scarcely be any question that what he has to say about the relation of the two societies in this work differs from his earlier treatments of the subject just because he has been led to reflect on the implication of the unfolding course of events in which both Latin Christians and pagans had such a stake. This would, indeed, be obvious even if the scattered remarks on those events found in the second part of the work did not echo the extensive treatment of Roman greatness we have just reviewed. By the same token, however, it is hard to speak of Augustine as a philosopher of history. Not only would the phrase have meant nothing to him; the fact is that his own understanding of the relation of the two societies was such that he was actually led in the circumstances to a fundamentally negative position on the only matter which practically concerned Latin Christians and pagans in his time—the immediate correspondence between worship of the true Deity and the peace and security of the empire.

This brings us to Augustine's place in the discussion of the material of classical *historia* to which Christians had been brought in his time. That place is easily described, but it is a complicated one. Augustine's special interests make him the logical successor of the pagan Latin historians both in that he is concerned with the subjective factors in the course of events of Rome's rise to greatness and because he is not driven for his own reasons to refer every such event to an immediate operation of divine providence. It is notable, as Professor T. E. Mommsen has pointed out, that he rejects such a notion as Orosius' that the ten plagues of Egypt foreshadowed the ten persecutions of Christians by pagan emperors (*History* VII.27) on the ground that it was rash to forecast the future of events (*City* XVIII.52.1-5). In another way, however, Augustine notably fails to speak to the central issue over which Christians and pagans divided in their interpretations of events. He does not really deny the operation of a special providence so much as he avoids it. Somewhere between his acknowledgment of the action of God in the works of the Christian emperors and his later statement that Christians accept the peace of the earthly city for the proximate value it has for human life, he has dismissed rather than resolved the issue which made the crisis to which he addressed himself what it was. The reaction of his contemporaries to his work was to show that it was not an issue which could be so easily, if so profoundly, overlooked.

6

The Crisis of the Christian Empire, II: Orosius to Gregory the Great

THE PERIOD of nearly two centuries between the time of Augustine and the pontificate of Gregory the Great saw the tide of disaster witnessed by the Latin West run ever more strongly. In A.D. 476 the military revolt in Italy was quelled by the government at Constantinople by the last of the barbarian resettlements in the West, and the Arian Ostrogothic kingdom of Ravenna was established. At the end of the century, the conversion of Clovis the Meroving and the Frankish conquest of the neighboring Arian tribes restored Gaul to Catholic unity, but further exploitation of the Church followed in its wake as one of the signs of the increasing social and cultural disintegration which marked the rule of the successor Merovingian dynasties. In the first half of the next century, the Emperor Justinian's expenditure of the resources carefully hoarded during the period of resettlement in a new policy of reconquest saw the restoration of imperial rule in Africa and Sicily but left only the shaky Exarchate of Ravenna to tend the fortunes of an Italy now devastated by war. When Gregory assumed, in A.D. 590, the episcopal office of the largely ruined and depopulated city which he still insisted on calling the Roman *respublica*, the Ravenna government was already proving its impotence by its failure to halt the infiltration of Arian Lombards not only into the valley of the river Po but as far south as the environs of Rome itself.

It is not surprising that the Latin Christianity of this period exhibits fewer contacts with the Greek Christian East than before. The christological controversy, which led to the Council of Ephesus in the year after Augustine's death at Hippo in A.D. 430 and convulsed the East throughout these centuries, seemed increasingly remote. The search for the meaning of the events of the time is the principal unifying theme which runs like a thread through the diverse liturgical and monastic, as well as the theological, remains of the period. Augustine merely stood at the brink of the crisis.

The enormous reputation of Augustine has not served his successors well. It is true that his greatness was recognized in his own time, and that he exercised an influence on his Latin Christian contemporaries greater than that of any other single individual. But he was still only one person in a generation which produced a number of important theological figures. His difficult relations with Jerome are well known. The incomprehensibility of his attitude toward Pelagianism has been noted in the case of the Gallo-Latin monastic theologians as well as in that of their Greek Christian associates. But if this is true it need not be expected that his highly individual view of the relation of the Church and the empire —his quite subtle avoidance of the logic which dominated the ideas of both the imperialists and their critics—would be any more comprehensible. It needs to be said with far greater clarity than it has often been said that on this central issue confronting the Latin Christian world of the time he stood as far to one side of the main theological developments of ideas as he did on many other issues.

It needs only a little reflection to see that there was a far more congenial interpretation of the crisis of the Christian empire open to Augustine's Latin Christian contemporaries than his own. The same logic which could lead to the expectation that the worship of the true God would bring peace and security to the once hostile empire could easily be used to argue that the disasters of the present time were not proof of the impotence of the true God but punishment for the sins of the Christian empire itself. In effect, the argument which Tertullian had advanced against the disasters besetting pagan Rome could be used against Christian Rome. Indeed, its use would not dissipate but would even augment that peculiar strength of character which has been perhaps equally engaging and distressing to later readers.

OROSIUS, THE "AUGUSTINIAN HISTORIAN"

It was part of Augustine's peculiar relationship to his successors that he was instrumental in focusing their attention on the very problem which he himself sought at all costs to avoid, that of the precise relation between the unfolding course of events and the operation of divine providence. This he did, in part at least, simply because of the arresting character of his own observations concerning the meaning of Rome's rise to greatness. But he also did it partly through his relations with his brilliant Hispano-Latin student, Orosius, to whom he committed the task of showing that the disasters which had befallen the pagan empires before the advent of Christianity were more calamitous than those which now beset the Christian empire. The result was Orosius' own *Seven Books of History against the Pagans,* which survived to provide not only the basis of Western medieval chronology but also the point of departure for early modern attacks on the integrity of Christian notions of a providence at work in the events of the past.

It is chiefly as a result of the work of Professor T. E. Mommsen that we have recently been made aware of the fact that Orosius' own views were far closer to those of the imperialists of the preceding century than to the more radical opinions of Augustine. Indeed, it was for adherence to a position which Augustine finally repudiated that Orosius' reputation ultimately suffered. Nevertheless, Augustine remains responsible for Orosius' work not only because he asked that it be written but for the more general but no less important reason that it stemmed from that perplexity about the meaning of present events which his own views could not finally repress.

Various questions arise regarding the dedicatory letter to Augustine which prefaces the work, but it is hard to miss the bitterness of the words in which Orosius says that he has

> obeyed your instructions . . . and may my achievement match my good intentions. . . . You indeed, have already assumed the burden of judging whether I was capable of what you intended, but I am content with the evidence of obedience alone, if I have done justice to that obedience by my will and effort (*History* I.*praef.*).

The probable cause of Orosius' bitterness—and here we follow Mommsen—is to be found in his later remark to the effect that he had not finished his work before the first ten books of the treatise *On the City of God* made clear to him that Augustine had proceeded without his help and persisted in issuing his work chiefly because the Bishop of Carthage had also encouraged him to do so (*ibid.*).

Their personal relations aside, the substantial difference between Orosius and Augustine shortly appears when the former defines his purpose as that of defending the notion that God has blessed the empire by reference to the disasters besetting the ancient empires:

> You bade me to reply to the empty chatter and perversity of those who, aliens from the city of God . . . charge that the present times are unnaturally beset with calamities for the sole reason that men believe in Christ and worship God. . . . [Thus] you bade me discover from all the available data of histories and annals whatever instances past ages have afforded of the burdens of war, ravages, and disease (*ibid.*).

Orosius admits that at the beginning "the disasters of my own times seemed to have boiled over and exceeded all usual limits," but that his study had convinced him "that the days past were not only as oppressive as those of the present but that they were more terribly wretched the further they were removed from the consolation of true religion" (*ibid.*). While the influence of Augustine's psychological interpretation of events appears when Orosius goes on to speak of the betterment of the human condition as the result of the spread of a faith which decries bloodshed, their fundamental difference is easily seen for what it is. At the very time that Augustine was beginning to move toward a more general interpretation of human ills through the amplification of the theme of the two cities, Orosius' attention remained fixed on the necessity of establishing a correlation of some sort between human betterment and the worship of the true God.

Orosius' true *historia* of past and present calamities is an attempt to establish just such a correlation. On a chronological basis, the work weaves together descriptions of the conflicts of the ancient Near Eastern empires, the conquests of Alexander and the warfare of his successors, Rome's rise to power in Italy, Rome's struggle with Carthage and later intervention in the affairs of the East, and the emergence of Augustus as heir to Caesar's power. To the Roman claim that the issue of these events was a rule of peace and happiness, he replies that they "bring happiness to a particular city, [but] weigh down the rest of the world with misery and accomplish its ruin" (V.1). By contrast, Orosius claims for the Christian empire a truer security and happiness. The influence of Augustine is here felt again when Orosius says, "I enjoy any country as my own because that native land which is my real home and the one which I love is not wholly on this earth," and adds, "I have lost nothing where I have loved nothing" (V.2). But for Orosius, the actualization of that true home is in the present age and "the blessings . . . which our ancestors never had in their entirety, the tranquillity of the present, hope for the future, and the possession of a common place of refuge" in an empire at once Christian, Roman, and humane (*ibid.*). His is a version of the imperial theology sobered by the events of the present but still recognizable in its essentials.

Orosius reveals more of his position as he turns to a discussion of the period from the advent of Christ to the present. Here he stoutly affirms that it was the birth of Christ which brought the Augustan peace. In a passage which takes for granted the universal citizenship of a rather later time, he declares that

it was by the will of our Lord Jesus Christ that [Rome] prospered, was protected, and brought to such heights of power, since to her [Christ] chose . . . to belong when he came, thereby making it certain that he was entitled to be called a Roman citizen according to the declaration made in the Roman census list (VI.22).

It is against this background that he places the persecutions which Christians suffered in the period which "granted a very peaceful reign to Caesar" (*ibid.*), and seeks to show that each of the persecutions was marked by a corresponding disaster to the empire in punishment for its refusal to acknowledge the true source of its security and happiness. But he also insists that since the time of Constantine the same issue has confronted the empire, since the "ever malignant opposition of the Devil to the true God from the beginning of the world" has now expressed itself through heresies such as Arianism and in unjust acts by Christian emperors, just as the power of God has also been manifest in raising up others to defend the faith and to do righteousness. In this period, too, judgment and reward have been meted out to those who rejected or accepted the issues of the time. Thus, in the case of Theodosius "heaven gave judgment between the side that humbly placed its hope in God alone even without the aid of man and the side that arrogantly trusted its own strength and in idols" (VI.36).

It is in this part of the work that Orosius' divergence from Augustine begins to appear more clearly. In his acceptance and elaboration of the relation between Augustus and Christ he now emerges as a true inheritor of the views of Lactantius, Ambrose, and Prudentius. It was precisely this relation that Augustine had never really accepted and from which he himself progressively turned away even in the part of *On the City of God* which Orosius knew at the time he issued his own work.

But Orosius is not blind to the depressing character of present events, and he has his own means of correcting the optimism of his predecessors. Even in the dedicatory letter, he already makes reference to the eventual coming of the Antichrist (I.*praef.*), and the above reference to the continuing work of the Devil is only one of many instances in which a sense of the encroaching power of evil pervades his thought. But it is at the end of the work that he chiefly concerns himself with the fact that before the final judgment, God's power will be withdrawn and the Devil have a last chance to exercise his influence among men in the coming of the Antichrist:

Alas a persecution by the Gentiles at some future time awaits us on our journey to freedom, until we cross the Red Sea—that is, the day of judgment, with our Lord Jesus Christ himself as our leader and judge. Those, however, who assume the role of the Egyptians, the power having temporarily been given them by the permission of God, will show their fury and persecute the Christians with the most grievous tortures. But all those enemies of Christ, together with their king, Antichrist, will be caught in the lake of eternal fire . . . and receive the lot of everlasting damnation (VII.27).

This is, of course, easily recognizable as part of the same interpretation of the sojourn in Egypt from which comes the notion that the ten plagues of Egypt refer to the ten persecutions of the pagan emperors, and that there need be no fear that such disasters will immediately be resumed. It is the view which is probably to be taken as the subject of Augustine's attack on such predictions of the future (*City* XVIII.52). And it must be confessed that his attack is justified when Orosius proceeds to insist that the Arian Christian invaders do not mark the beginning of these events, interestingly altering Augustine's own argument about the Christianity of the Gothic tribes to one which emphasizes the fact that their incursions have been "checked, confined, incorporated, or annihilated with little bloodshed" (*History* VII.43). But on the larger point of Orosius' sense of the catastrophe impending over the age, his exploration of this theme is the thing which brings his work alive as an interpretation of the whole of human events from the perspective of his own time. If he shares the belief of the imperialists in the possibilities opened through the relation of Christ and Augustus, his view of the Christian empire in particular is one which regards it as a brittle structure precariously balanced on the brink of the disasters to come.

Quite apart from his wider influence as a purveyor of *historia* in Christian dress into medieval and modern times, then, Orosius is immediately of interest for the light he sheds on the currents of thought with which he was involved. The divergence of the views of the person so long regarded as the Augustinian historian from those of his master shows the persistence throughout the period of the notion of the correspondence of earthly blessings and true worship which the Bishop of Hippo Regius was virtually alone in seeking to avoid. But Orosius' emphasis on the precarious character of the present also serves to foreshadow the reactions of those of his successors who could not maintain even his expectations and for whom there was only one theme out of the past which seemed to make sense in the light of the deepening crisis—the theme of punishment merited by those who had failed to respond to the possibilities thrust upon them. Orosius not only witnesses to the persistence of past assumptions but anticipates the conclusions which were to be drawn from them.

SALVIAN AND THE TERTULLIANIST REVIVAL

It is perhaps extravagant to speak of the Latin Christian response to the disasters which now began to befall the West as involving a Tertullianist revival. There is little evidence of any conscious return to the great Carthaginian theologian of an earlier era, or of a reversal against the trends of thought which had more recently stimulated Latin Christians under the influence of their Greek Christian contemporaries. On one single count, however, the phrase is eminently justified. Throughout the period of optimism now effectively closed by recent happenings, the theme of the necessity of facing the issues confronting men in the unfolding course of events had never been absent from even the most sanguine of Latin Christian estimates of the new possibilities open to the empire. But in the face of increasing disasters this theme assumed an importance it had not had since Tertullian employed it in denouncing the sins of pagan Rome. In its new form it differed from his in the crucial respect that it applied not to pagan but to Christian Rome. To this Rome it held out no possibility of peace and security to come, but only the final mercy of God for those who responded to the meaning of the time.

The evidence of this theme survives for the most part in liturgical remains later preserved in the Carolingian era—where a starkness inappropriate to the spirit of that later time readily betrays their earlier origin. The classic contemporary expression of the theme, however, is the eight books of the unfinished treatise *On the Governance of God* written about A.D. 440 by Salvian, presbyter of the church at Marseilles. Salvian wrote within a few years of Augustine's death and not long after Orosius produced his *History*. His vastly different appraisal of the times is, however, easily explained by the different perspective afforded him by his position in Gaul, the highway of the invasions.

Salvian's work opens with a bitter denunciation of those who react to their sufferings by questioning God's governance of the present age. When even Platonists and Stoics—indeed, "all men, even those not of our faith"—acknowledge God's rule, he asks, "how can he at present be thought indifferent or unconcerned?" (I.1.) When the pagan Romans "for the sake of spreading Roman imperial power scorned their private wealth" and Greek philosophers "with greed for glory despoiled themselves" of their possessions, he pursues, it ill behooves Christians to complain when "in this life they possess the joys of their faith and will obtain the rewards of blessedness in the next" (I.2). But the central point on which he insists is that those who complain have dangerously failed to see that the sufferings of the present are punishments visited on his people by God. They are a revelation of God's rule over the present age: "while God governs us, he judges us, because his governance is his judgment" (I.4). Salvian's argument simply draws a different conclusion from the very logic employed by those he attacks. The events of the time are not ground for complaining of God's impotence but reason—a very real and pressing reason—for examining the implications of his power.

The occasion for Salvian's work was the attitude of the wealthy Latin Christians of Gaul. But the work goes far beyond anything that one can imagine as an immediate answer to their complaints. It includes not only an extensive elaboration of Salvian's main argument but its use as the basis for an interpretation of the unfolding events of the time. Thus it is only after an extended examination of scriptural proofs of God's rule that he returns to his main point on the basis of the text "Behold I am with you all days, even to the consummation of the age" (Mt. 28:20). Those who complain against God, he charges, are themselves guilty of ingratitude for God's care;

> Do you, ungrateful men, say that he who is "with" us unceasingly has no care or regard for us? What does he do when "with" us? Is he "with" us to scorn and neglect us? And how can it happen that he is "with" us in our piety and neglects us in our impiety? . . . We give a fine interpretation of God's love if we falsely say that he constantly neglects us, while he himself says that he never does neglect us (II.2).

The crux of the matter is, of course, that God's care is exercised in judgment as well as blessing. Here Salvian develops at length the words of Nathan in attacking David for the murder of Uriah the Hittite, "Behold I will raise up evil against you out of your own house" (II Kings 12:9). Is it not obvious, Salvian asks, that these words explain the present events of which people complain?

> Do you not see that the eyes of God were never absent even from that secret sin through which David once fell? Learn from this that you are always seen by Christ; understand and know that you will be punished, and perhaps very soon, you who . . . think that your acts are not seen by God (II.4).

Indeed, Salvian holds out no immediate hope for his contemporaries even if they do repent. He reminds them that the reward of David's repentance was "that he was not condemned to eternal punishment," not that he received "pardon in this world" (*ibid.*). Moreover, he cautions his contemporaries not to rely on a different judgment at the end from that which they are now receiving. Contrasting the text, "You have sat on the throne, you who judge justice" (Ps. 9:5) and "He shall judge the world in equity" (Ps. 95:13), he notes that God here merely "distinguishes the time element between the present and future judgments" (*Governance* II.6). This is the hard lesson which he calls on those who think that God has deserted them to learn before it is too late for them to do so.

It should be obvious by now that Salvian's work is another example of the Latin interest in organizing and presenting an argument in order to confront the readers with the immediate issues thrust upon them by the circumstances in which they stand. It is this interest which now explains the inconsistent but effective weaving together of various strands of earlier thought in the further argument that, if a Christian claims God's favor on the ground that "I am not doing these things now," he must remember that present virtue will not reverse the divine judgment on past vice (III.11), while anyone who claims the Christian name as a defense against punishment for the past must understand that "neither does he possess faith who lacks faith nor does he who tramples on the mandates of Christ believe in him" (IV.1; cf. III.11). Salvian's concern is to anticipate what he imagines will be the defensive reactions to his main point rather than to explore the implications of his individual statements.

But it is this same interest which leads to the next argument, which seeks to undercut the claim of the wealthy Latin Christians of Gaul to some consideration for having maintained the social structure and for being poorly served, as they believe, by the desertion of their unappreciative slaves (IV.3 ff.). No sinner, Salvian insists, need think to claim favor on the ground of God's love. The fact that "God loves us more than a father loves his son" is, he admits, shown in his giving of his own Son for us. Indeed, "any man would be acting unjustly if he caused his own son to be killed for the sake of his worst slaves." Thus, God's love is so great that his justice "seems almost a kind of injustice" (IV.10). But one must not be deceived by this, since the apparent difference between God's love and his justice is made up by the fact that he allows us to pay the debt which we owe him through our answering love or through death (IV.10-11). God's love cannot be invoked to lift our present sufferings, nor yet denied if "he allows us to bear these evils because we deserve to suffer them" (IV.12). The purpose of this difficult argument is simply to sweep away another attempt to obscure the meaning of the events of the present with which Salvian seeks to confront his readers.

It is this same purpose which, finally, explains the form in which Salvian refurbishes an earlier classical image of the stalwart barbarian in the light of such evidence as he possesses of the contrast between barbarian virtue and Roman vice (IV.13-19) and even excuses the heresy of the Arian barbarians "who err through the acceptance of a seemingly correct opinion" (V.2). In view of their virtues, he pursues, it is not surprising that many prefer barbarian rule to the oppressive laws of Rome (V.3-9). Salvian's purpose is once again to confront his readers with the disintegration of the Gallo-Latin society, not as a ground for complaint but as a call for repentance from its members. Thus he concludes: "Deny yourself, therefore, lest you be denied by Christ; disown yourselves in order that you may be received by Christ; lose yourselves lest you perish. . . . You will not be completely set free by God unless you yourself denounce yourself" (V.11).

Specific instances of Salvian's use of Tertullian's *Apology* have frequently been noted. They extend from such a general theme as pagan acceptance of God's rule, Tertullian's "soul naturally Christian" (*Apology* VII), used by Salvian to bring Christian doubt into perspective (*Governance* I.3), to such a specific point as Tertullian's discussion of pagan beliefs that Christians sacrifice children at the Eucharist (*Apology* VIII), which Salvian merely cites to suggest the depraved religious practices of such pagans who would have assumed such a thing possible (*Governance* IV.17). But the broader similarities between Salvian and Tertullian should not be overlooked. It is scarcely irrelevant that Salvian organizes and presents his material as a means of winning recognition of the issues of the time, or that he finds in the calamities of the present the judgment of God manifest against the disobedience of Rome—they are hallmarks of Tertullian's work. The difference, of course, is that Salvian finds inspiration in Tertullian for calling Christian Rome to repentance in the name of the God whose judgment is now being rendered against his own people. But Salvian still remains a witness to the way in which continuing disasters recalled Latin Christians to a more somber side of their nature than that reflected in the works of the imperial theologians of the century past.

Salvian's praise of the stalwart barbarian—in fact, his contrast between the virtues of the invaders and the vices of the Romans—

carries him on into the further description of the events of his time. His description is an important source for modern students of the period, though he has been frequently attacked for prejudice. Quite rightly so—though the ground of his prejudice is not always recognized for what it is. In fact, these sections also belong to his appeal to the Christians of the day to recognize the signs of the times:

> The resources of former times have gone. We are already poverty-stricken, yet we do not cease to be spendthrift. . . . The causes of corruption are not in enticements, as with other men, but in our hearts. Our wickedness is in our minds, so that the loss of wealth does not move us to amend our way of life. We proceed to sin through love for evil things (VI.9).

What follows is a picture of a world hopelessly mad, overrun by disaster but blind to its true state. The barbarians have entered Italy and crossed into Spain, but while "the lot of the Spaniards is indeed changed, their wickedness is not changed" (VI.12). In Africa, too, "the barbarian peoples were sounding their arms around the walls of Citra and Carthage, and the Christian population of Carthage still went mad in the circuses and reveled in the theaters" (*ibid.*). Indeed, Salvian claims that in Gaul he has witnessed, at the sack of Trier, "honored old men, tottering Christians, the ruin of their city imminent" following their accustomed habits of luxury (VI.13). But in all this detail, Salvian's main point is never far away. In these sections in particular, the reminiscence of Tertullian's interpretation of the calamities of his time is unmistakable (*Apology* XVIII). The account of these happenings, Salvian insists, is given

> in order to prove that all these calamities which we have suffered have been borne not by lack of God's providence or through his neglect, but rather in justice and judgment. . . . We have suffered them because no portion of the Roman world or the Roman name, however gravely struck by heavenly punishment, was ever fully corrected (VI.16).

Rome thus remains essentially what it always has been—the same subject for God's punishment of which Tertullian spoke.

It is this point which he now presses home in ever further instances of the vicious character of the times. Prefacing his account by reiterating that "they who know God's Law and neglect it sin more than they who in ignorance do not act according to the Law" (VII.1), he now comments on the barbarians to the point directly opposite that which he made on this same basis earlier. The vice and heresy of the invaders serves God as a means of revealing the critical nature of the times: "We are judged by God with immediate judgment and therefore a craven race has been raised up for our destruction and shame" (VII.12). But even this final remedy has little hope of success. In initiating a catalogue of the immoralities of Africa—an account which reflects in part the popular judgment on those provinces—he piously issues the hope that "eternal evils will not succeed and follow the punishment of temporal evils" (VII. 15). But he later observes that, in fact, none of the calamities of the past "have corrected any people who bear the Roman name" (VII.17). His view is, thus, not merely a parallel but a continuation of that of Tertullian. The sins for which Christian Rome is now punished are the very sins for which pagan Rome was punished earlier. Christian Rome, the implication clearly is, is precisely the same as pagan Rome.

We do not know where Salvian would have carried his argument beyond this point, since the work breaks off in the midst of his catalogue of the vices of the Africans (VIII.5). Indeed, it is hard to see where the argument could have been carried by a person in his position, or how he could conceivably have given any concrete meaning to his call to denounce what his entire generation had been educated to regard as the virtual equation of the terms "Christian" and "Rome."

It will not have been overlooked that Salvian's insistence on the irreformability of the Romans, Tertullianist though it may be in inspiration, is based in part on references to the confusion of the mind through fascination with earthly things (cf. VI.9) which are reminiscent of the Augustinian analysis of the human problem. Moreover, it can be even more certainly stated that Salvian's analysis of the happenings of his time reflects the emphasis which Latin

Christians had perforce to lay on the unfolding course of events in the wake of not only Orosius but of the imperial theologians with whom he aligned himself. Indeed, when Salvian's picture of a world gone virtually mad is attacked for its obvious biases, such attacks are as much a witness to the realistic and circumstantial character of his account as to the special reasons for his undertaking it. With his work we have passed far beyond Orosius' already rather threadbare optimism. But the actual grip of the course of events remains to make the work almost an appendix to his *historia*. In any case, it should be evident that it was that course of events itself rather than any abstract convictions of his own which undergirds Salvian's return to Tertullian's emphasis on the immediate judgment of God as the clue to the meaning of his time. His is another step in the process by which Latin Christians were forced to seek theological meaning in the events of their time.

GREGORY THE GREAT

The years which separate Salvian and Pope Gregory the Great contain much of interest to us. In conscious imitation of earlier Greek historians and in continuity with Ammianus Marcellinus, Procopius produced his firsthand account of the African and Italian campaigns of Justinian. In the West, Gregory of Tours' *History of the Franks,* for all its deficiencies of language and method, is of great importance for the light it sheds on the new matrix of the affairs destined to come into its own with the formation of the Frankish empire of Charlemagne. But the only theological significance of Procopius' work lies in the contrast between its neutral approach to events and the theological claims about to be made for the cosmic significance of the reduced empire based on Constantinople; and Gregory of Tours' naïve notions of divine providence do not lead him into any such search for the meaning of events as we have seen in Orosius and Salvian. By contrast, the work of Gregory the Great stands out as the final phase of the

Latin Christian attempt to understanding the crisis of the Christian empire.

Gregory's life is a saga. Son of a Roman senatorial family, he left the monastic community he had established in his villa above the city to serve as one of the seven deacons of Rome, its ambassador to the imperial court, and finally Bishop of Rome. His brief episcopate, from A.D. 590 to 604, was conservative in intention, dedicated simply to the fulfillment of required duties. In the circumstances of the time, however, even such an intention was a radical one. It led Gregory to attempt to recover and use the revenues owing from the land-holdings of the Roman Church but often appropriated by the imperial officials in Sicily and the Merovingian rulers of Gaul. It led him to contest the use of the title "Ecumenical Patriarch" by the Constantinople bishop as threatening the jurisdictional equality of the five patriarchal sees. It led him to seek, not only as Roman bishop, or Metropolitan, but as Patriarch of the West, to arrest the decay of the pastoral office throughout his jurisdiction, and in particular to attack the exploitation of the episcopate in Merovingian Gaul.

With the same curious combination of conservative intention and radical implementation, Gregory assumed what was virtually the civil as well as the ecclesiastical rule of the Roman *respublica* and entered into negotiations with the Lombards without reference to the Exarcate at Ravenna. In the same way, when apprised of the possible conversion of the pagan Saxon king of Kent, he acted independently of the Merovingian bishops to seek the establishment of an English Church dedicated to his own reforming views.

These last proved later to have been his most important acts. The first provided precedent for his successors in flaunting imperial authority to establish the relations with the Carolingian House which ultimately brought a new world into being in the ruins of the West. The second created that remarkable group of men, the highly trained and intensely Roman clergy of the English Church who forged those relations even before it was convenient or appropriate for the Roman Church to acknowledge them. Thus, while

Gregory probably died thinking himself a failure, the effect of his work could be summarized by the Venerable Bede as being that "though he was not an apostle to others, yet he is so to us; for we are the seal of his apostleship in our Lord" (*Ecclesiastical History of the English Nation* II.1). But Bede also embodied the eschatological motive which drove the great pope to his hopeless task when he wrote that "his body was buried in the church of the holy Apostle Peter . . . to rise one day in the same body in glory with the rest of the holy pastors of the Church" (*ibid.*).

In striking contrast to the interest shown in his life has been the curious disinterest in Gregory's thought. Indeed, Gregory has been the victim of several common assumptions about his time. The fact that he employed the relics of the Roman Church as a kind of negotiable security in his dealings with the Merovingians—and on one occasion explained his refusal to part with relics of the Apostle Peter by reference to the mysterious death of workmen repairing his tomb—has been endlessly cited to show the superstition of the time rather than being recognized as evidence of the pope's diplomatic skill. On the other hand, the fact that Gregory's views differ in crucial respects from those of Augustine has as frequently been used to prove his theological inadequacies rather than as cause to reconsider the extent of Augustine's influence in his own time. There could scarcely be a stranger characterization of the real man than this.

Gregory's understanding of the Christian life, which was the central focus for all of his thought, places him in the ranks of those Latin Christians who found inspiration in the Greek Christian ascetical tradition rather than in the Tertullianist rigorism which we have just seen revived in the work of Salvian. His relationship to Augustine consists in his recognition of his distinguished predecessor as a mediator of that tradition. Among a relatively few passages which suggest concrete Augustinian influence is that in which Gregory explains in his *Dialogues,* in which he sets forth evidence of God's action in the lives of holy men in Italy, that after Adam was "driven outside of himself by his sinful act, he was no longer able to perceive the joys of heaven" and that the men "born . . . of his flesh into the darkness of exile" now only hear from others "that there is a heavenly country, that angels are its citizens, and that the spirits of the just live in company with them"(IV.1). Here also he adds that the Word became incarnate and the Spirit was sent to enable us "to receive new life in order to believe those truths of which we as yet had no knowledge through experience . . . (being) no longer in doubt about the existence of invisible things" (*ibid.*). The notion of Adam's exclusion from a heavenly country is certainly at least indirectly Augustinian, despite the fact that it is the Platonic theme of forgetfulness which chiefly engages Gregory's attention.

It is the latter theme, however, which introduces the more characteristically Gregorian ideas that form the structure within which this particular section of the work is set. Indeed, it is an elaboration of this theme that provides one of the more striking descriptions of present existence found in all the works, in which Gregory says:

> As the present age approaches its end, that of eternity looms nearer, manifesting itself by ever clearer signs. Is it not true that in this age it is impossible for us to see each other's hearts? Why then should we not compare this age to a dark night, and the life to come to the light of day? In the transitional hour before the sunrise, when the night comes to an end and the new day is about to begin, darkness is somehow blended with light until the remaining shadows of the night are perfectly absorbed in the brightness of the coming day. In this way the end of the age merges with the beginnings of eternal life (IV.43).

Moreover, it is the sense of the mysteriousness of present existence that this passage suggests which is later united with the theme of the judgment to come when Gregory declares that

> if we do not sincerely forgive injuries, we shall have to give a second account of the sins for which we have already done penance and experienced the joy of forgiveness. So while we are enjoying the days of grace, while our judge holds off the sentence and the examiner of our sins awaits our conversion, let us soften our hardened hearts with teaching and practice of charity and kindness toward our neighbor. Then we can be sure

that, if we offer ourselves during life as victims to God, we will not need to have the saving victim offered for us after death (IV.62).

Students of later doctrinal developments will, of course, recognize this as one among the passages in which Gregory anticipates later views of purgatory. This witness to Gregory's influence should not be allowed, however, to obscure the immediately more important fact that this particular aspect of his teaching witnesses to a fusion of the notion of the growing enlightenment of the soul by the eternal light now dawning—his inheritance from Greek Christian ascetical theology—with the continuing influence of the Latin Christian emphasis on Christ as the source of hope for men at the judgment to come. Placed in its context, Gregory's thought is not a deficient version of Augustine's ideas but a novel fusion of the theological sources which had combined in various ways in the work of Latin Christians since the fourth century.

In view of his active career, it is not surprising that Gregory's serious discussion of the Christian life is confined to the sermons of the period of the episcopate and to the enormous thirty-five books of the *Moralia on Job,* a commentary begun at some point before his assumption of episcopal authority curtailed such activities. While it is not possible here to deal with this extensive work, it is easy enough to see how appropriate was its subject to the expression of Gregory's views. Prefaced with a standard exposition of the classic three senses of the Scriptures, literal, allegorical, and moral, the work is actually devoted to a typological treatment of the suffering of Job as foreshadowing both the sufferings of Christ and those which his elect are to undergo as the purification necessary in this age to the perfection of the age to come. The often noticed elevation of the moral above the allegorical meaning of the scriptural account is, in effect, the result of a fusion of the Alexandrian exegetical tradition with that more common in Latin circles no less characteristic of Gregory's work than his anticipation of later views of purgatory—and no less indicative of later trends of scriptural interpretation in the medieval West.

The specific connection in which we need to refer to the

Moralia has to do with the prefatory reference which Gregory makes to the circumstances in which he was led to abandon his monastic retreat for service in the world. Writing to his friend Leander, Bishop of Seville, he deplores the fact that at the very time that "as I then vainly believed I had come out naked from the shipwreck of human life" he was forced to act because "now that the end of the world is at hand, and the times disturbed by increasing evils, we ourselves . . . have become involved in outward cares" (*praef.*1). At the same time we may cite the important passage in a letter in which Gregory replied to the congratulations sent by the Bishop of Carthage on his assumption of episcopal office, in which he is more explicit as to the "outward cares" now confronting him:

> I confess that sorrow strikes through my soul from contemplation of this office. The weight of it is indeed heavy, considering that the Lord when about to depart to receive for himself a kingdom, and giving talents to his servants, says in Luke, "Trade ye till I come" (Lk. 19:13). In view of this responsibility I tremble, and look to the returning of the master of the house, after receiving his kingdom, to take account of us. But with what heart shall I bear his coming if, from the trading I undertook, I render him no gain? (*Letters* II.47.)

Taken together, these two passages relate the two recurrent themes, of the progress of the soul toward perfection and the account shortly to be rendered of every man's deeds, to Gregory's own life. On the one hand, he seeks a respite from the cares of the world which, as the theme of shipwreck shows (cf. Methodius, *Symposium* IV.1), marks his inheritance from the Greek Christian ascetical tradition. On the other hand, the life of action to which he has been called is not merely relevant to salvation (cf. Basil of Caesarea, *Letter* 299) but a responsibility on which that salvation depends. Nor do the themes remain distinct, since Gregory's retreat is into a life of preparation for coming perfection, while the responsibilities thrust upon him are those of a servant who awaits his Lord's return.

The startling aspect of these passages is Gregory's belief that he had been called to deal with the affairs of the Roman Church literally in the last days of the present age. While he himself often speaks of the judgments God has rendered in specific instances of human behavior, he is chiefly preoccupied with the natural calamities of the time as foreshadowing the actual destruction of the physical cosmos—as unmistakable signs of the approaching end. For example, in the *Dialogues* he instances the increase of underwater volcanic activity off Sicily as evidence that "with the end of the world approaching it seems that the openings to hell are enlarged in order to receive the greater number of lost souls . . . (for) God has made these fires to appear on the surface of the earth in order to correct the minds of men" (IV.36).

But the natural catastrophes which chiefly engaged his attention as a clue to the coming end are those which had befallen the already ruined imperial city that was his episcopal see. Gregory of Tours in recording the flooding of the Tiber and the plague which subsequently caused the death of Gregory's predecessor, Pope Pelagius, and precipitated his own election, sets down an address to the people to heed the signs of time with penitence and change of heart, which certainly embodies in substance Gregory's reaction to these specific events (*History* X.1). But Gregory's *Dialogues* gives a more general account of his views when relating a prophecy regarding Rome's end made by Benedict of Nursia on the eve of the Lombard siege. "Rome will not be destroyed by the barbarians," Gregory records Benedict as saying, "but will be shaken by tempests and lightenings hurricanes and earthquakes, until finally it lies in its own ruins." Gregory then comments that this prophecy is being fulfilled in the present: "We have seen the walls of Rome crumble and its houses in ruins, . . . its churches destroyed by violent storms, and its delapidated buildings surrounded by their own debris." Moreover, he has no doubt that Benedict understood God's purposes and revealed them:

All who follow the Lord wholeheartedly are living in spiritual union with him. As long as they are still weighed down by the body, however, they are not actually united with him. It is only to the extent they are one with God that they know his hidden judgments. . . . Since even holy men cannot fully grasp the secret designs of God during this present life, they call his judgments inscrutable (Rom. 11:33). At the same time they understand his judgments and can even pronounce them with their lips (Ps. 118:13) (*Dialogues* II.16).

But Gregory also associates the catastrophes befalling Rome with the judgments of former days. In the *Homilies on Ezekiel* he applies the image of the melting of a pot whose contents have already boiled away (Ezek. 24:3) to Rome's present and former handling by God:

Of this city it is well said, "The meat is boiled away and the bones thereof." For where is the Senate, where are the people? . . . All the pomp of the dignities of the present age is gone. Yet even we who remain are daily smitten with the sword, are daily crushed with innumerable afflictions. Thus it is said, "Set the pot also empty on the coals." . . . Rome is as it were empty and burning. The ruin spreads and we see the very buildings perishing. . . . The pot itself is being consumed in which were first consumed the flesh and bones (*Homilies* II.6).

Thus the catastrophes befalling Rome are not entirely distinct from the disasters of the past. Both manifest the judgment of God. But the fact of the physical ruin of the ancient capital—the visual reality of it, however actually caused—means to Gregory that the end of the present age is now truly at the door.

We are here obviously at the source not only of Gregory's ideas but of his actions—his attempt in the few brief years given to him to fulfill the obligations of a Roman bishop at the end of the age. This is nowhere clearer than in the letter he wrote to accompany his embassy to the king of Kent (*Letters* X.67). Confronting Ethelbert with the possibility of achieving the favor with God which Constantine himself acquired as a protector of the true faith, he counsels haste. Indeed, he observes, "the end of the present age is already close at hand," and notes that this is manifest from the extraordinary physical events: "changes of the air, terrors from heaven, and seasons contrary to the accustomed order of times, wars, famine, pestilences, earthquakes in many places," though for reasons of pastoral diplomacy, conscious conviction, or profound hope for his project, he also adds that the end "will not come in our days, but after our days all will follow." The letter can be read in various ways. But it is clear that both his exhortation to haste and the hope for success which he holds out perhaps as much to himself as to the king are equally grounded on the notion of approaching end. It is that end and the judgment that it heralds which was the focus of his thought and of the ground of the actions which he undertook and exhorted others to undertake with him.

Gregory can be compared and contrasted with his predecessors in various ways. His thought is of the subtler type that we have found in Orosius. His presentiment that events are driving the present age to its end breeds in him a spirit more akin to that of Salvian. But he stands alone on the one point of his direct eschatological pronouncements. The strange thing about Gregory, which no one who reflects on the debt which the modern world owes to its medieval past can fail to recognize, is that it was his sense of the coming end which informed the ideas and policies that were integral to the creation of an era which he himself did not believe would ever exist.

THE END OF THE CRISIS

It is easy and proper to dismiss the notion of a "fall of the Roman empire." Constantinople remained a free city and the bearer of the idea of a Christian empire until the fifteenth century. The vision of such an empire remained to goad Westerners to action throughout the medieval period and survived into modern times. But it is still important to speak of the ending of the crisis of the Christian empire with which we have here dealt. That end was, indeed, brought about by the very events already mentioned. The withdrawal of imperial power from the West slowly erased from memory the frightening reversal of the Christian hopes which had been inspired by the recognition of the Church. The survival of the idea of a Christian empire in the West served a new function in the course of events—that of a goal to be sought more than of a reality whose actual character had presented cruel problems for Christian faith.

But if events themselves brought the crisis to an end, they did not erase from history the crisis itself nor curtail its influence. The crisis remains as a further evidence of the continuation of the logic inherent in the Gospel, whereby the unfolding course of events must command attention as the arena in which God's purposes in his dealings with his creatures are manifest. Moreover, it was at this point that the subject matter of the entire course of human events, and the political and psychological aspects of those events, which had hitherto been the peculiar province of *historia*, became matters of crucial importance to Christian faith. The Christian appropriation of this problem was, moreover, to have the greatest consequences for the future. The notion of the providential action of God which informed all Christian considerations of this now vastly extended panorama of events was to provide the medieval Christian West with the central feature of its understanding of its own inner disputes and external actions—in the crusades, in the struggles of popes and feudal monarchs, and in the disastrous period of the loss of papal power and prestige which heralded the rise of the European national powers as independent entities in their own right. And the same notion was to provide the background against which those disenchanted with the structure of Christian doctrine were eventually to seek in classical *historia* the means of describing what they could not fail to recognize as the unitive course of events in terms that freed them from the necessity of relating all to the immediate design of God.

In all this, the figures we have considered in this chapter played a crucial part—and, concretely, a more important part than did the looming figure of Augustine of Hippo, who has for so long and for many reasons rightly dominated our memory of those times. Important as Augustine is in the debate over the meaning of present events into which Christians were led by the crisis, his final response to the crisis was to see it as nothing but another instance of the weakness of the earthly city. It was his less distinguished contemporaries, Orosius, Salvian, and Gregory, who saw that the enmeshment of the fortunes of Christianity and Rome could not be so easily dismissed. In the end their apprehensions about the end— and, in particular, those of Gregory—were proved false by events, as had been those of Israel's prophets and even the Apostle Paul before them. But it was the actions which they undertook—and, again, those of Gregory in particular—which created an age that they did not foresee. It is hard to imagine that Augustine's resigned outlook would have led him to perform the prodigious works which Gregory's forced him to attempt. Indeed, when we consider Augustine's profound influence on medieval and modern culture, we must remember that it was inexplicable apart from Gregory's very different understanding of the issues confronting men in the events of the time.

Epilogue

LIKE its predecessor in this series, the present study has concerned itself with a theme of modern theological significance as it appeared in early Christian theology. In dealing with the theme of "history," it has been necessary to examine both the efforts of Patristic writers to read the continuing purposes of God in the events of their time and the ways in which those efforts eventually led the Latin writers of the period after the recognition of the Church to confront events formerly regarded as the province of classical *historia*.

This study began with what was perhaps a caricature of a present tendency to contrast a "biblical" concern with history to the detriment of an understanding either of the Patristic concern with the course of events in which God's purposes are manifest or of the way in which this concern illuminates the modern theological situation which gives rise to this very tendency. Supposing that we have been successful in clarifying the problem of "history" as early Christian writers understood it, we may now mention some general considerations which have to do with the modern theological situation in which the question of "history" looms so large.

One such consideration concerns the nature of early Christian theology itself. That theology was a theology in the specific sense that it sought to develop the implications of Christian belief in the particular circumstances created by the existence of the world of

Greco-Roman ideas. As such, it was nearer in style and intent to the largely unsystematic efforts of the pagan philosophers than to the theological or philosophical systems with which we are familiar in the medieval and modern West. To be sure, the early Christians were led, in the prosecution of their work, into speculations of the subtlest and most profound sort, as the views of the Greek Christian Platonists, both Alexandrian and Cappadocian, show only too clearly. But as Professor Norris has shown in the preceding volume, even the subtlest and most profound of these speculations is never far removed from substantive issues created not from a concern to achieve a comprehensive picture of reality but from an immediate interest in discerning the specific implications of Christian belief for the world of ideas of which that belief was now a part. Much of our current bemusement over the thought of the early Christian centuries is attributable to our ingrained assumption that the writers of this period must have been concerned with the kind of theological or philosophical systems—whether biblically or rationally based —with which we are familiar.

This peculiar characteristic of early Christian theology has been visible here in several ways. We have seen that the writers from Justin to Origen, authors of the axial ideas, so to speak, on which all later developments turned, pursued their work on the assumption of God's present activity. It was one of the central points of Christian belief which informed all that they said. If they found it increasingly difficult to invest the full course of human affairs with ultimate significance, and if this was also the case with their successors in the theological flowering of the fourth and succeeding centuries, this was the case because of the nature of the cosmological and anthropological issues which confronted them rather than because of any doubt regarding the reality of that activity.

But the occasional character of early Christian theology is even more clearly revealed here in the simple fact that commitment to the present activity of God implied an openness to the unfolding course of events which was in principle incapable of systematization. This fact was grasped most clearly by the Latin Christians of the fourth and succeeding centuries, inheritors as they were of earlier efforts to explain Christian belief in the face of Rome's understanding of its own destiny and confronted as they were with the novel and unsettling events of their own time. Their work was no less *theological* than that of their Greek Christian contemporaries. Rather it extended the front, so to speak, of the Christian struggle to explain their faith to the intellectual world of the time which was the essential characteristic of Patristic theology. The Latin Christian invasion of the province of *historia*—indeed, the revival of the problems of *historia* on theological grounds—is a witness to the nature of early Christian theology in all of its aspects.

But another major consideration must be introduced at this point. This is the place of early Christian theology as the watershed between the classical and the later Western world of ideas. The repopulation of the Church from the Mediterranean society of the Greco-Roman period involved the conversion of the community of faith into a social phenomenon in its own right. In the same way, the effort to set forth the implications of Christian belief for the Greco-Roman world of ideas involved both the introduction of new rational considerations into the theological realm and the emergence of Christian belief as a force in the main stream of intellectual endeavor. Neither of these processes was ever seen for what it was in the early Christian period. The memory of the pagan roots of classical society and culture remained to create a tension in early Christian minds between two distinct spheres of reality, Church and world, even after the recognition of the Church. Nor did these processes ever subsequently achieve the perfection sometimes suggested. The formation of a Christian society in medieval Europe had not been accomplished before the autonomous national societies began to emerge—and emerge in part out of the power struggle of clerical and lay leadership. Similarly, the notion of a "medieval synthesis" in Christian thought remains a myth to be corrected by the evidence of the emergence of nontheological if not entirely "secular" ideas long before the so-called Renaissance. Nevertheless, modern society and culture are what they are because of their birth in a period marked by a complex combination of acceptance and rejection of Christian institutions and ideas.

Thus it is that the early Christian discussion of the purposes of God manifest in the unfolding course of events is not only a subject in its own right but the background against which must be set both the writing of theologically oriented medieval chronicles and the eventual emergence of a new interest in the study of events —an interest which is as much the result of the appropriation of a Christian interest in the unitive meaning of events as it is a result of dissatisfaction with the Christian tendency to find the purposes of God immediately manifest in those events. This is only one of the ways in which early Christian theology forms the background of the modern intellectual enterprise, but it is easily one of the most striking.

As such, the early Christian treatment of history, both as course of events and as *historia,* serves to illuminate the place where we stand today. The peculiar character of this aspect of early Christian theology can be described as involving, at least in the Latin Christian reactions to the crisis of the Christian empire, another instance in which the logic operative in the life of Israel and the primitive Church was once again applied to the unfolding course of events. It culminated in yet a fourth to be added to Professor Guthrie's three outbreaks of the peculiarly Judeo-Christian response to the divine purpose manifest in human affairs. This outbreak involved intellectual consideration of a sort never before introduced. But if it is to be faulted, it is not for its departure from some scriptural norm as much as for its almost slavish adherence to earlier Christian expectations of the future as somehow requiring to be substantiated from the course of events. Both Augustine's virtual repudiation of the significance of a Christian empire and Gregory the Great's hasty proclamation of the end of the present age are cases in point.

Modern Christians are in more difficult straits. They are witnesses to a further unfolding of events which has seen Christianity emerge as a force in the creation of a society and culture which early Christian writers never foresaw, and which has also witnessed the emergence of new social and cultural developments not contemplated by the leaders of Christendom and only now recognized in their peculiar character as products of both the acceptance and the repudiation of Christian ideas. Modern Christians confront a culture which is at once aware of the eventful character of human existence and uncertain of what to make of it. They also confront a form of *historia* which is alternately bemused by the meaning of the total course of events and concerned to abandon the pursuit of that meaning in either empirical or existential descriptions of human happenings.

In these circumstances, frequent reference to Christian interest in "history" is of little use. Unless we are prepared to abandon the Gospel as a proclamation of what God is "up to" in the unfolding course of events—and our increasing knowledge of that Gospel, itself a product of the very historical concern which characterizes our time, makes this increasingly difficult to do—there is no escape from the difficult task of saying precisely what we mean by that proclamation as it affects our understanding of the new events of which we are witnesses. To undertake that task is to involve ourselves not only with the current bemusement over eventful existence as such but with the modern discussion of the nature of *historia* as well. Indeed, to undertake that task is to resume the early Christian discussion of history in both of its senses and in circumstances at least as perplexing as those in which that discussion developed. In the very nature of the case, our study of that discussion has not told us what we are to say about the new events of which we are witnesses so much as to reveal the issues with which we must deal.

Bibliography

General Bibliography

Texts and Translations. Among collections of the writings of the period, three should be mentioned as being the most readily available. Of these the most comprehensive is still that edited by J. P. Migne, *Patrologiae cursus completus,* 390 vols. (Paris: 1844 ff.), now being fully reprinted. Results of a still unfinished project to provide more adequate texts are the so-called Berlin Corpus, *Die Griechischen christlichen Schriftsteller der ersten Jahrhunderte,* 41 vols. (Leipzig: Hinrichs, 1897 ff.), now slowly being re-edited; and the so-called Vienna Corpus, *Corpus Scriptorum Ecclesiasticorum Latinorum,* 80 vols. (Vienna: 1866 ff.), on which work is now being resumed. Translations given throughout are based on the most readily available of those listed in the various bibliographical notes in order that they may be more easily identified by those who wish to pursue these matters further.

General Works. Among the most useful means of access to Patristic writings are patrologies, which combine comments on the various works with extensive bibliographical data. That of J. Quasten, *Patrology,* 3 vols. to date (Westminster, Md.: Newman, 1950 ff.), unfortunately has not reached the Latin writings of the fourth and following centuries. On these writings, see the more condensed B. Altaner, *Patrology,* trans. H. C. Graef (Freiburg: Herder; Edinburgh-London: Nelson, 1958). The most useful general history of early Christian thought in English is J. N. D. Kelly, *Early Christian Doctrines* (New York: Harper, 1960). Now in paperback is A. von Harnack's classic but outdated *History of Dogma,* trans. N. Buchanan (New York: Dover, 1960). Among histories of the early Christian period, the first four volumes of the monumental Fliche-Martin, *Histoire de l'Église* are available as J. Lebreton and J. Zeiller, *History of the Primitive Church* (London: Burns, Oates and Washbourne, 1942) and J. R. Palanque *et al.*, *The Church in the Christian Roman Empire* (London: Burns, Oates and Washbourne, 1949).

There is a small literature which deals in a general way with the matters considered here. The aforementioned work of Collingwood, *The Idea of History*, is responsible for revolutionizing the whole discussion of both ancient and modern *historia* and takes account of the place of Christianity in its "history." Two works which deal with the destiny of Christian eschatology in the early Church are the aforementioned W. Kamlah, *Christentum und Geschichtlichkeit*, and K. Löwith, *Meaning in History* (Chicago: University of Chicago, 1949). Both proceed on the assumption that there is a biblical norm to be followed in this matter, though Kamlah's norm is roughly that of R. Bultmann and Löwith's roughly that of O. Cullmann. Many of the other works mentioned earlier have a more general bearing on the entire subject than we have had occasion to note but cannot in the circumstances be cited again.

R. L. P. Milburn's Bampton Lectures, *Early Christian Interpretations of History* (London: A. and C. Black, 1954), is virtually unique in surveying the historical methodology of Christian writers throughout the period. It thus examines an aspect of our study which has been curtailed in the interest of the broader question of the reception of the eschatological theme of the Gospel in the early Christian period.

Modern Historia. Since we are here indirectly concerned with the origin and character of modern historical study, at least some attention must be paid to the considerable literature on this matter.

An important treatment of the formative stages of and constitutive forces at work in modern historical study, now available in paperback, is H. Butterfield, *Man on His Past* (Boston: Beacon, 1960). The relation of modern theological developments and the emerging historical consciousness is treated in O. Chadwick, *From Bossuet to Newman: The Idea of Doctrinal Development* (Cambridge, Eng.: University Press, 1957). The classical period of modern historical work is examined in G. P. Gooch, *History and Historians in the Nineteenth Century*, now in paperback (Boston: Beacon, 1959). A post-Collingwood treatment of the problem of historical knowledge is H. Bloch, *The Historian's Craft* (New York: Knopf, 1959). The views of Collingwood and Bloch are compared in T. A. Roberts, *History and Christian Apologetic* (London: SPCK, 1960), chap. 1. A series of brief essays, many dealing with the changing perspectives of modern historical study, is the work of the historian of medieval Germany, G. Barraclough, *History in a Changing World* (Oxford: Blackwell, 1957).

One of the more useful ways into recent discussions of history is through anthologies of the sort represented by H. Meyerhoff (ed.), *The Philosophy of History in Our Time* (Garden City: Anchor Books, 1959) and F. Stern (ed.), *The Varieties of History* (New York: Meridian Books, 1956). The existence of various works of this sort is a witness to current recognition of the importance of the subject and of its perplexing character.

We must end by mentioning a few of the recent works which seem to have most to say about the issues to which attention is directed here. The collected essays of C. Dawson, in J. J. Julloy (ed.), *Dynamics of World History* (New York: Sheed and Ward, 1956), contain a wealth of suggestive material on the place of religion in general, and of Christianity in particular, in the study of the course of events. M. C. D'Arcy's *The Meaning and Matter of History: A Christian View* (New York: Farrar, Straus and Cudahy, 1959) examines matters more directly related to the theological issues of the Patristic period. H. R. Niebuhr's *Resurrection and Historical Reason: A Study in Theological Methodology* (New York: Scribners, 1957) has a far more general bearing on the gulf between modern historical assumptions and Christian claims regarding the uniqueness of events than its quite specific topic might suggest. Finally, H. I. Marrou's *The Meaning of History*, Eng. trans. R. J. Olsen (Baltimore: Helicon, 1966) offers a fresh treatment of the nature and importance of historical knowledge by a scholar who is esteemed in both classical and Patristic circles.

Bibliographical Notes

1 THE PRIMITIVE GOSPEL AND CLASSICAL HISTORIA

The Primitive Gospel. The views of G. von Rad to which reference is made are found in his *Theology of the Old Testament,* Vol. II, trans. D. M. G. Stalker (New York: Harper, 1966), esp. pp. 99 ff., 263 ff. Much of my own thinking has been influenced by views of my colleague Harvey H. Guthrie, Jr., available in part in his *God and History in the Old Testament* (New York: Seabury, 1960) and his Winslow Lectures, *Wisdom and Canon: Meanings of the Law and the Prophets* (Seabury-Western Theological Seminary, 1966). See also W. Pannenberg, "Redemptive Event and History," in C. Westermann (ed.), *Essays on Old Testament Hermeneutics,* trans. J. L. Mays (Richmond, Va.: Knox, 1963).

Radically different approaches to the issue raised by the rediscovery of the "eschatological" motif in Jesus' preaching associated with the name of A. Schweitzer are to be found in O. Cullmann, *Christ and Time,* trans. F. V. Filson (Philadelphia: Westminster, 1950), and R. Bultmann, *History and Eschatology* (New York: Harper, 1962). The present situation is surveyed in the important article of K. Stendahl, "Biblical Theology, Contemporary," *Interpreter's Dictionary of the Bible,* Vol. I (New York and Nashville: Abingdon, 1962).

On the importance of distinguishing Paul from "Paulinism," see esp. J. Munck, *Paul and the Salvation of Mankind,* trans. F. Clarke

(Richmond, Va.: Knox, 1959), esp. chaps. 3, 7; and K. Stendahl, "The Apostle Paul and the Introspective Conscience of the West," *Harvard Theological Review*, LVI, 199-215. A contrary view is taken in W. D. Davies, *Christian Origins and Judaism* (Philadelphia: Westminster, 1962), chap. 8, "A New View of Paul—J. Munck: 'Paulus und die Heilsgeschichte.'" The newly discovered Tura fragment of Origen's *Commentary on Romans* now serves to place his work with Augustine's *Letter to Simplician* as a crucial turning point in the history of "Paulinism."

Classical Historia. A classic study of *historia* in ancient and modern times which takes account of the impact of Christianity is R. G. Collingwood, *The Idea of History* (Oxford: Clarendon, 1946). C. N. Cochrane established the medical theme in Thucydides in his *Thucydides and the Science of History* (London: Oxford, 1929) and dealt with the relation of Christianity to historical and other aspects of classical intellectual endeavor in his *Christianity and Classical Culture* (now in paperback—New York: Galaxy, 1957). M. L. W. Laistner's *Greater Roman Historians* (Berkeley and Los Angeles: University of California, 1963) is useful for the light it sheds on the peculiarities of the Latin practice of the Greek discipline. No notice need be taken of the notion that the Greeks had a "cyclic" view of history. The notion seems to be an exegesis of Augustine's attack on the philosophical *circuitus temporum* (*City of God* XII.18) or of earlier Christian amusement over pagan speculations regarding the recurrence of events (Origen, *Against Celsus* IV.68; Tertullian, *On the Soul* XXX). But neither have to do with *historia* as such.

The unique features of the Latin outlook are nicely discussed in R. H. Barrow, *The Romans* (Baltimore: Pelican, 1949) and E. Auerbach, *Mimesis* (Garden City: Doubleday-Anchor, 1957), chap. 3, "Fortunata." The views of B. Otis on Vergil are found in his magisterial *Virgil: A Study in Civilized Poetry* (Oxford: Clarendon, 1964) and his "Virgil and Clio: A Consideration of Virgil's Relation to History," *Phoenix*, XX, 59-75. It will be noted that the two traditions of the spelling of the poet's name persist. An important discussion of the special characteristics of the Roman religious tradition is found in F. Altheim's sometimes rather speculative *A History of Roman Religion*, trans.

H. Mattingly (London: Methuen, 1938), esp. Bk. II, chap. 5, "The Roman Form" and Bk. IV, chap. 4, "The Religion of the Augustan Age."

Translations of the Greek and Latin works mentioned are all available in the *Loeb Classical Library*.

2 THE GOSPEL AND LATER GREEK PLATONISM: JUSTIN TO ORIGEN

The serious need for an up-to-date study in English of the Greek Christian writers of the second and third centuries for the general reader has been met by two recent works: R. A. Norris, Jr., *God and World in Early Christian Theology* (New York: Seabury, 1965), the first volume of the present series, and H. Chadwick, *Early Christian Thought and the Classical Tradition* (Oxford: Clarendon, 1966). Among works which bear directly on our own particular interests, it is to be hoped that J. Daniélou, *Message Évangélique et Culture Hellénistique* (Histoire des doctrines Chrétiennes avant Nicée, II) (Paris: Desclée, 1961) will soon follow its predecessor into English translation. The relation of the work of these writers to that of their fourth-century successors is treated in B. Otis, "Cappadocian Thought as a Coherent System," *Dumbarton Oaks Papers*, XII (Cambridge, Mass.: Harvard University, 1958), 97-124, and "Nicene Orthodoxy and Fourth-Century Mysticism," *Actes du IIe Congrès International des Études Byzantines* (Belgrade: 1964), II, 475-484.

The only comprehensive collection of these writings in English is still the uneven translation in Vols. I, II, and IV of *The Ante-Nicene Fathers* (Grand Rapids, Mich.: Wm. B. Eerdmans, n.d.). Some of these writings are available, in whole or in part, in the better translations in Vols. I and II of *The Library of Christian Classics* (Philadelphia: Westminster, 1953, 1954). Now available in paperback is G. W. Butterworth's *Origen on First Principles* (New York: Harper, 1966), a translation with introduction and notes.

Justin and His Immediate Successors. The last full-scale study of Justin in English is the now virtually unobtainable E. R. Goodenough,

The Theology of Justin Martyr (Jena: Frommannsche, 1923). Justin's philosophical connections are debated in G. Andresen, "Justin und der mittler Platonismus," *Zeitschrift für die neutestamentliche Wissenschaft*, XLIV (1952-53), and R. Holte, "Logos Spermatikos: Christianity and Ancient Philosophy according to St. Justin's Apologies," *Studia Theologica*, XII (1958). On the tradition of scriptural interpretation represented in Justin, see Daniélou, *From Shadows to Reality*, trans. W. Hibberd (London: Burns and Oates, 1960). There are some suggestive remarks in B. Lindars, *New Testament Apologetic* (Philadelphia: Westminster, 1961). Future study of Irenaeus will proceed on the basis established in such works as A. Benoit, *Saint Irénée: Introduction à l'étude de sa théologie* (Paris: Presses Universitaires de France, 1960), A. Houssiau, *La Christologie de saint Irénée* (Louvain: Publications Universitaires de Louvain, 1955), and F. Sagnard, *La Gnose Valentinienne et le Témoignage de saint Irénée* (Paris: Vrin, 1947).

Clement of Alexandria and Origen. The development of pagan allegorical methods and its influence on the Alexandrian and other Christian writers of the period is studied in R. M. Grant, *The Letter and the Spirit* (New York: Macmillan, 1957). Two works of R. P. C. Hanson, *Origen's Doctrine of Tradition* (London: SPCK, 1954) and *Allegory and Event* (London: SCM, 1959) study the theological implications of the scriptural methods of Clement and especially Origen. An important study of Clement on similar lines is C. Mondésert, *Clément d'Alexandria* (Paris: Aubier, 1954). Clement's philosophical views are treated by E. F. Osborn, *The Philosophy of Clement of Alexandria* (Cambridge, Eng.: University Press, 1957). See also the articles of R. P. Casey, "Clement and the Two Divine *Logoi*," *Journal of Theological Studies*, 1924; "Clement of Alexandria and the Beginnings of Christian Platonism," *Harvard Theological Review*, 1925. From the vast literature on Origen, it must suffice to mention the general introduction of Daniélou, *Origen*, trans. W. Mitchell (New York: Sheed and Ward, 1955). Works which touch on our special interests in various ways include H. Cornélis, "Les fondements cosmologiques de l'eschatologie d'Origène," *Revue des sciences philosophiques et théologiques*, 1959, and H. Koch, *Pronoia und Paideusis* (Berlin: De Gruyter, 1932). Certain remarkable insights into both of the Alexandrian teachers are found in E. Molland, *The Conception of the Gospel in Alexandrian Theology* (Oslo: Proceedings of the Norwegian Academy of Science, 1938).

3 THE GOSPEL AND ROMAN ESCHATOLOGY: TERTULLIAN AND CYPRIAN

Writings of Tertullian and Cyprian are available in rather uneven English translations in Vol. III of *The Ante-Nicene Fathers*. The selection found in *The Library of Christian Classics* (Vol. V: *The Early Latin Fathers*) unfortunately lacks Tertullian's *Apology*. No translator can fairly be faulted for failure to come to terms with Tertullian's elusive Latin.

The Latin writers of the period have received surprisingly little attention of late. For introductory studies the following may be consulted: P. de Labriolle, *History and Literature of Christianity from Tertullian to Boethius*, 1st French edition trans. H. Wilson (London: Kegan Paul, 1924); H. von Campenhausen, *Fathers of the Latin Church*, trans. S. Godman (London: A. and C. Black, 1964). W. H. C. Frend, *The Donatist Church: A Movement of Protest in Roman North Africa* (Oxford: Clarendon, 1952) treats the whole phenomenon of Latin sectarianism in grand style, though its estimate of local, non-Latin factors is different from that assumed here. The kind of linguistic study which seems to point the way to a new understanding of the issues of early Latin theology is found in C. Mohrmann, *Études sur le latin des Chrétiens*, Vol. I (2nd ed.; Rome: Edizioni di Storia e Letteratura, 1961). Otis' "Virgil and Clio: A Consideration of Virgil's Relation to History" suggests lines along which such a new understanding might develop.

Tertullian. The philosophical elements in Tertullian's thought are treated in part in Norris, *God and World in Early Christian Theology*, chap. 4. The well-known propensity of Tertullian for Stoicism, which we have noted in the particular instance of the use of the concept of the interval or *diastema* of time, but which pervades his whole treatment of the acquisition of virtue, needs thorough re-examination in the light of recent studies of the eclectic character of contemporary Greek philosophy and of its use by such Latin philosophers as Cicero and Seneca.

R. Braun, *Deus Christianorum: Recherches sur le vocabulaire doctrinal de Tertullien* (Paris: Presses Universitaires de France, 1962) is an important first step in the application of Tertullian's language and style to the study of his theology. The relation of Tertullian's views of the Scripture to the structure of his thought is examined in H. Karpp, *Schrift und Geist bei Tertullian* (Gütersloh: Bertelsmann, 1955).

Cyprian. The most recent general study of Cyprian's theology is still that of A. d'Alès, *La Théologie de St. Cyprien* (Paris: Beauchesne, 1922), though his treatment of the problem of schism figures very largely in G. Bardy, *La Théologie de l'Église: de saint Irénée au concile de Nicée* (Paris: Editions du Cerf, 1947). The whole question of the growth of episcopal authority, in which Cyprian also figures, is examined in W. Telfer, *The Office of a Bishop* (London: Darton, Longman, and Todd, 1962). A widely accepted view of the references to the Papacy in *Unity* IV, namely that Cyprian qualified his early view of the Roman bishop as embodying the unity which Peter had initially reflected in the course of his dispute with Pope Stephen over the rebaptism of schismatics, is that developed by M. Bévenot in his *St. Cyprian's De Unitate, Chap. 4, in the Light of the Manuscripts* (Rome: Analecta Gregoriana, 1938), summarized in the introduction to his translations of Cyprian's treatises in *Ancient Christian Writers,* Vol. XXV. Few things would be more useful today, however, than a thorough review of Cyprian's "Tertullianism" in the light of our growing understanding of the Latin elements in the thought of "the master."

4 THE PROBLEM OF "RECOGNITION": EUSEBIUS AND HIS AGE

The writings of Lactantius are available in English in Vol. VII of *The Ante-Nicene Fathers,* and selections from those of Eusebius and Ambrose in Vols. I and X of *A Select Library of Nicene and Post-Nicene Fathers,* Series II (Grand Rapids, Mich.: Wm. B. Eerdmans, n.d.). Eusebius' *History* appears with useful introduction and notes in H. J. Lawlor and J. E. L. Oulton, *Eusebius* (London: SPCK, 1927); Ambrose's oration is to be found in Vol. XXII of *The Fathers of the Church* (New York: Fathers of the Church, Inc., various dates). Prudentius' poetry is available in the Loeb Classical Library and in Vol. LII of The Fathers of the Church. The surviving work of Ammianus Marcellinus is also available in Loeb.

General studies of the period now available in paperback include the aforementioned Cochrane, Christianity and Classical Culture and S. Dill, Roman Society in the Last Century of the Western Empire (New York: Meridian Books, 1958). An illuminating discussion of the problems involved in interpreting Constantine's religious policies is also available in paperback in A. H. M. Jones, Constantine and the Conversion of Europe (rev. ed.; New York: Collier Books, 1948). The relation of Christianity and continuing paganism is treated in the various articles in A. Momigliano (ed.), The Conflict between Paganism and Christianity in the Fourth Century (Oxford: Clarendon, 1963). See also P. Courcelle, Les lettres grecques en Occident (rev. ed.; Paris: Boccard, 1948).

A brief survey of the development of the imperial policy regarding Christians which does much to recover the true picture of the sporadic character of the persecutions and the varieties of Christian attitudes toward them is R. M. Grant, The Sword and the Cross (New York: Macmillan, 1955). In support of our contention that not even the "toleration" which preceded and succeeded the great persecution of Diocletian and his successors prepared Christians theologically for the startling reversal of policy which the emergence of Constantine as a force in public affairs heralded long before his assumption of sole rule in A.D. 324, see Frend, Martyrdom and Persecution in the Early Church (Oxford: Basil Blackwell, 1965). Far more space than is here available would be needed to deal with this question—one of the most interesting and important issues of current research and debate.

Eusebius. A recent full-scale treatment of Eusebius is D. S. Wallace-Hadrill, Eusebius of Caesarea (London: Mowbray, 1960). Recent studies of Eusebius' view of the work of Constantine are found in F. E. Cranz, "Kingdom and Polity in Eusebius of Caesarea," Harvard Theological Review, XLV, 47-66, and T. E. Mommsen, "St. Augustine and the Christian Idea of Progress: The Background of the City of God," Medieval and Renaissance Studies (Ithaca: Cornell University, 1959), pp. 265-298, both of which contain useful further bibliographical notes. The relation of Eusebius' view to his Trinitarian theology views is examined in G. H. Williams, "Christology and Church-State Relations in the Fourth Century," *Church History*, XX/3, 3-33; XX/4, 3-26.

The Greek Christian theological concerns which curtailed interest in Eusebius' view in the East are treated in their evolution from the work of the Alexandrian School in the aforementioned articles by Otis, "Cappadocian Theology as a Coherent System" and "Nicene Orthodoxy and Fourth Century Mysticism." A particularly nice illustration of the temper of the later Greek Christian Platonic mind regarding the political realm is found in *Letter* 299 of Basil of Cappadocian Caesarea (available in the *Loeb Classical Library*) which consoles a high civic official who had entered the monastic community founded on the Cappadocian estates for having to accept a responsible but dangerous involvement in affairs of the world unlike the remote existence in which the perfection of the soul is more likely to be found.

The Latin Imperial Theologians. Sketches of Lactantius, Ambrose, and Prudentius are found in Labriolle, *History and Literature of Christianity from Tertullian to Boethius*. Their views on matters treated here are discussed in the articles of Cranz and Mommsen, whose bibliographical references should also be consulted in this connection. A comprehensive treatment of Christian views of Rome is found in E. Peterson, *Der Monotheismus als politisches Problem* (Leipzig: De Gruyter, 1935).

Special studies available in English are almost all concerned with Ambrose. The most extensive biography is F. H. Dudden, *The Life and Times of St. Ambrose*, 2 vols. (Oxford: Clarendon, 1935). J. R. Palanque, *Saint Ambroise et l'Empire Romain* (Paris: 1933) should be consulted for further bibliography. Of considerable interest as background for the case of the Altar of Victory is A. Alföldi, *A Conflict of Ideas in the Late Roman Empire: The Clash between the Senate and Valentinian I* (Oxford: Clarendon, 1952).

5 THE CRISIS OF THE CHRISTIAN EMPIRE, I: AUGUSTINE

The most comprehensive collection of Augustine's writings in English is in Vols. I-VIII of *A Select Library of Nicene and*

Post-Nicene Fathers, Series I. The crucial first part of the *Letter to Simplician,* as well as a modern rendering of *On the True Religion,* is included in *The Library of Christian Classics* (Vol. VI: *Augustine: Early Writings*). In the same series is Vol. VIII, *Augustine: Confessions and Enchiridion.* Among other translations of *On the City of God,* that of M. Dods is available in various forms. The abridgment of the work in V. J. Bourke, *St. Augustine: The City of God* (Garden City: Image Books), usefully preserves the argument of the original by summarizing omitted sections.

A useful introduction to the issues which Augustine faced is C. Dawson, "St. Augustine and His Age," in M. C. D'Arcy (ed.), *Monument to St. Augustine,* now in paperback as *St. Augustine: His Age, Life, and Thought* (New York: Meridian Books, 1957). See also G. Quispel, "Time and History in Patristic Christianity," in *Man and Time* (New York: Bollingen Series XXX.3), pp. 85-107. A work which has done much to correct the overemphasis on Augustine's early life, which he himself did much to create by *Confessions,* is F. van der Meer, *Augustine the Bishop,* trans. B. Battershaw and G. R. Lamb (New York: Harper, 1965).

Indispensable for a more extensive study of the aspects of Augustine's thought treated here are F. E. Cranz, "*De civitate dei* xv.2 and Augustine's Idea of the Christian Society," *Speculum,* XXV, 220 ff., and his "The Development of Augustine's Ideas on Society before the Donatist Controversy," *Harvard Theological Review,* XLVII, 255 ff., as are also the aforementioned Mommsen, "St. Augustine and the Christian Idea of Progress," his "Augustine and Orosius," *Medieval and Renaissance Essays,* 325 ff., A. Lauras and H. Rondet, "La thème des deux cités dans l'oeuvre de S. Augustin," Rondet *et al., Études Augustiniennes* (Paris: Aubier, 1953), 97 ff., and W. Kamlah, *Christentum und Geschichtlichkeit: Untersuchungen zur Entstehung des Christentums und zu Augustins "Burgerschaft Gottes"* (Stuttgart und Köhl: Kohlhammer, 1951).

Works of related interest include R. H. Barrow, *Introduction to St. Augustine: The City of God* (London: Faber and Faber, 1950); J. Burnaby, *Amor Dei: A Study of the Religion of St. Augustine* (London: Hodder and Stoughton, 1938); and J. Guitton, *Le temps et l'éternité de Plotin et S. Augustin* (2nd. ed.; Paris: Aubier, 1955). The work of G. Ladner, *The Idea of Reform* (Cambridge, Mass.: Harvard University, 1959), chap. 5, surveys Augustine's general thought and provides further bibliography from an almost inexhaustible supply.

Cappadocian Theology. It would have been foolish even to suggest by a few parenthetical citations the extent and complexity of Augustine's relation to the Cappadocian fathers. The cosmological basis of Cappadocian Trinitarianism is set forth in Gregory Nazianzus, *Theological Orations* and Basil of Caesarea, *Against Eunomius*; its broader ramifications for the nature of embodied existence in Gregory of Nyssa, *On the Making of Man* and *On the Soul and the Resurrection*—works found in Vols. VII, VIII, and V, respectively, of *A Select Library of Nicene and Post-Nicene Fathers,* Series II.

Perhaps the most useful introductions to Cappadocian thought in English are the aforementioned articles of Otis. On the crucial issue of the defection of the mind, see J. Gaïth, *La conception de la liberté chez Gregoire de Nysse* (Paris: Vrin, 1953). On the subject of time, see the bibliographical references in my own "The Conversion of *Diastema* in the Patristic View of Time," in R. A. Norris, Jr. (ed.), *Lux in Lumine: Essays to Honor W. Norman Pittenger* (New York: Seabury, 1966). J. Callahan has pioneered in studying the relation of Augustine and the Cappadocians in his articles "Greek Cosmology and Cappadocian Theology," *Dumbarton Oaks Papers*, XII, 31-57nn., and "Basil of Caesarea: A New Source for St. Augustine's View of Time," *Harvard Studies in Classical Philology*, LXIII, 437-454. A startling number of aspects of their relationship remain to be considered at this writing.

6 THE CRISIS OF THE CHRISTIAN EMPIRE, II: OROSIUS TO GREGORY THE GREAT

The *Fathers of the Church* series contains English translations of Orosius (Vol. L), Salvian (Vol. III), and Gregory, *Dialogues* (Vol. XXXIX). See also the translation of Orosius, with introduction and notes by I. W. Raymond, *Records of Civilization*, Vol. XXVI. It is a commentary on recent interest in Gregory that the only translation of the *Moralia on Job* remains that in *The Library of the Fathers*, Vols. XVIII, XXI, XXIII, XXXI (1844-50). The only translation of Gregory of Tours' *History* which does not omit Gregory's "Coronation Address" is O. M. Dalton, *The History of the Franks by Gregory of Tours* (Oxford: Clarendon, 1927). The numbering of Gregory's *Letters* followed here is that of Migne, used in Vols. XII and XIII of *A Select Library of Nicene and Post-Nicene Fathers.* More commonly cited in scholarly works is that of P. Ewald and L. Hartmann, *Gregorii I Papae Registrum Epistolarum,* 2 vols., in *Monumenta Germaniae Historica,* which also provides a comparative list of the several orderings of the letters.

Among many background works, F. Lot, *The End of the Ancient World,* rev. ed. and intro. G. Downey (New York: Harper, 1961) is now available in paperback form. S. Dill, *Roman Society in Gaul in the Merovingian Age* (London: Macmillan, 1926) is a classic. See also M. L. W. Laistner, *Thought and Letters in Western Europe A.D. 500-900* (rev. ed.; London: Methuen, 1957). Of great importance is the recent P. Courcelle, *Histoire littéraire des grandes invasions germaniques* (Paris: Études Augustiniennes, 1964), as well as the paperback edition of C. Dawson, *Religion and the Rise of Western Culture* (Garden City: Image Books, 1958). The aforementioned work of Labriolle is less useful for this later period of Latin Christianity.

Orosius. The aforementioned articles of Professor T. E. Mommsen are indispensable points of departure for any study of Orosius. His bibliographical references will serve to show how slight has been the attention recently paid this figure. The present treatment of Orosius departs from Mommsen's in its emphasis on the continuing influence of Augustine in his work.

Salvian. Salvian has, if anything, received less general attention, though there are now available a larger number of adequate studies. An important treatment of Salvian's background is that of N. K. Chadwick, *Poetry and Letters in Early Christian Gaul* (London: Bowes and Bowes, 1955). His preoccupation with the disasters of the time is the subject of R. Thouvenot, "Salvien et la ruine de l'empire romain," *Melanges de l'école francais de Rome,* XXVIII, 154-163. The specific influence of Tertullian is studied in J. Waszink, "Tertullien et Salvien," *La Musée Belge,* XIX, 39-43.

Gregory the Great. The only extensive English work is F. H. Dudden, *Gregory the Great: His Place in History and Thought,* 2 vols. (London: Longmans, Green, 1905). Still valuable is the briefer P. Batiffol, *Saint Gregory the Great*, trans. J. L. Stoddard (London: Burns, Oates and Washbourne, 1929). With most modern studies of Gregory's career, both accept substantially the ninth-century work of John the Deacon. My own remarks, brief as they must be, have tried carefully to skirt such difficult problems as Gregory's position as "abbot" of St. Andrew's on his return from the East, his patronage of the Benedictine *regula*, and his role in the liturgical renewal later associated with his name—all aspects of the Gregorian saga which need careful re-examination. Of modern studies of Gregory's thought, mention should be made of L. Weber, *Hauptfragen der Moraltheologie Gregors des Grossen* (Freiburg i.d. Schweiz, 1947). See also M. Frickel, *Deus totus ubique simul* (Freiburg: Herder, 1956), J. P. McLain, *The Doctrine of Heaven in the Writings of St. Gregory the Great* (Washington: Catholic University, 1956). My own views owe much to those of the Rev. Dr. Milton M. Gatch, whose unpublished B.D. thesis, "The Latin Spirit from Gregory the Great to Charlemagne" (Episcopal Theological School, Cambridge, Mass., 1960) is only the first instance of my indebtedness.